Smokeless powder, nitro-cellulose, and theory of the cellulose molecule

John B. Bernadou

BIBLIOLIFE

SMOKELESS POWDER, NITRO-CELLULOSE,

AND

THEORY OF THE CELLULOSE MOLECULE

BY

JOHN B. BERNADOU,

Lieutenant, United States Navy

FIRST EDITION

FIRST THOUSAND

NEW YORK

JOHN WILEY & SONS

LONDON: CHAPMAN & HALL, LIMITED

1901

PREFACE

FOR purposes of comparative study, the writer has brought together in the present volume a series of papers, by various investigators, upon the composition of cellulose and the properties of explosives prepared therefrom. He has supplemented these with an account of experiments made by himself; and from the whole has drawn certain conclusions as to the possible ultimate chemical composition of cellulose and the nitro-celluloses.

While the general development of war-material from the mechanical and metallurgical standpoints—the production of ordnance and armor—is so largely identified with progress in the useful arts in the United States, yet, until very recently, but little has been accomplished in our country in the way of improvement in explosives. Within the last few years, however, a particular form of smokeless powder has largely supplanted the old black and brown powders for military uses; and the last decade of the past century has witnessed the virtual abandonment of a propellant that has held its place in war, with comparatively little modification, for four hundred years.

This new smokeless powder, which is adapted for use in arms of all calibres, is prepared from a particular type of colloid nitro-cellulose. Such an extension of the employment of this latter body from its original use for detonating purposes, to its new use as a progressive explosive, has attracted general attention, and led to a more careful and extended study of the nitrocelluloses in general. It is with the view of further extending such study and of possibly preparing the way for the introduction of future improvements in progressive explosives that this book has been prepared.

Before presenting it, the author wishes to express his thanks to certain eminent scientists for the privilege that they have courteously afforded him of making his own translations of certain portions of their works upon explosives: to Professor D. Mendeléef, of Russia, for his paper entitled "Pyrocollodion Smokeless Powders"; to M. Vieille, of the French Service des Poudres et Salpêtres, for his article upon the nitration of cotton; and to M. Bruley, of the same service, for a similar paper. Thanks are due also to Messrs. Longmans, Green & Co. for the privilege kindly extended of making certain extracts from Messrs. Cross and Bevan's valuable work, "Cellulose," published by them.

Finally, the author wishes to express his indebtedness to Dr. Alfred I. Cohn, of New York, for the care he has bestowed upon the reading of the proof of this book at a time when the writer's absence from the United States on active service afloat prevented his giving the matter the personal care and attention it otherwise would have had; and for his preparation of a comprehensive index.

U. S. S. "Dixie," April 24, 1901.

TABLE OF CONTENTS

CHAPTER I

CHAPTER II

CHAPTER III

CHAPTER IV

APPENDIX I

APPENDIX II

APPENDIX III

APPENDIX IV

SMOKELESS POWDER

CHAPTER I

ORIGIN

THE discovery that cellulose, by treatment with nitric acid, is converted into a highly inflammable or explosive body was made during the first half of the nineteenth century. The action of nitric acid on starch was investigated to some extent in 1833 by Braçonnot, who found that a very rapidly burning material was produced, and which he named xyloidine. Pelouze further investigated this substance in 1838, and also studied similar bodies prepared from paper, linen, etc., which he held to be identical with the one from starch.

In 1846 Schönbein discovered that cellulose in the form of cotton, when immersed in nitric acid, freed from the acid excess, and dried, was converted into a highly explosive compound. This latter substance, subsequently known as gun-cotton, constitutes the base of modern smokeless powders.*

---

* The name " gun-cotton," as originally employed, was generic for all varieties of the more highly explosive nitro-celluloses prepared from cotton.

On its first appearance gun-cotton was hailed by ordnance experts as a smokeless substitute for gun-powder, and extended series of experiments were conducted to prove its adaptability to the requirements of war. The combined efforts of chemist, powder-maker, and artillerist failed, however, to secure such a control of its combustion as would enable it to be safely employed, in charges of a given weight, to develop a uniform bore-pressure with standard projectiles in guns of a given calibre. After the occurrence of a number of detonations, unlooked for and more or less disastrous, its use was abandoned. Nevertheless, the study of the composition, properties, and methods of production of gun-cotton and kindred bodies continued to be systematically prosecuted, the theory of nitro-substitution was evolved, and the knowledge of the applicability of the new materials to military requirements extended. But more than forty years were to elapse from the time of the first experiments before a thoroughly reliable smokeless powder, free from all tendency to detonation, producing minimum erosion, of good keeping qualities, and of maximum propulsive effect, was to be obtained.

To trace the various steps of progress in the determination of the properties of gun-cotton is exceedingly difficult. It is primarily difficult for the reason that the base-material under investigation possesses an organic structure; and because the resultant nitrated product varies in chemical composition according to strength and temperature of the acids employed in its preparation, their water content, duration of reaction, and temperature at which the reaction is conducted. It is difficult secondarily for the reason that the ultimate product of nitration is either resolvable, by treatment with certain solvents, into different subcomponents, or else is capable of direct preparation in a form soluble in one or another solvent; and because certain industries, sciences, and professions—the manufacture of explosives, of fabrics, photography, surgery—have required the development of special forms of material and demanded special lines of research.

The existence to-day of a very large number of unclassified names to denote the different varieties of nitro-cellulose, serves as an illustration of the necessarily involved and complex nature of such investigations as have been made for the purpose of determining its composition, and of the incompleteness of these investigations. The confusion in nomenclature that has arisen is attributable to the fact that the formula for cellulose, and therefore for the cellulose nitrates, not being established, investigators in different countries started in independently to determine simultaneously both the properties of these compounds and their chemical constitutions. Matters became further involved through the efforts to translate the accounts of the work of one investigator into the language of another.

With the view of avoiding confusion in the future it may be well to anticipate somewhat here, to indicate the origin of the various names applied to forms of nitro-cellulose, to define and classify them, and to indicate such of them as will be employed hereafter in the body of the present work ot denote those distinct varieties that possess significance from the standpoint of explosive effect.

NOMENCLATURE

Names may be divided into classes, according to origin, as follows:

1.—Those devised by discoverers to denote new chemical compounds. Thus, xyloidin, from ξύλος, wood; pyroxylin, from πῦρ, fire, and ξύλος, wood.

2.—Those implying uses to which special forms of the material are applied, as gun-cotton, collodion-cotton.

3.—Those originating in references to the theory of nitro-substitution; thus, nitro-cellulose, mono-, di-, tri-, tetra-, penta-, etc., nitro-cellulose.

4.—Names based upon the physical characteristics of the material, as "soluble nitro-cellulose," "insoluble nitro-cellulose," "friable cottons" (Vieille).

5.—Names obviously incorrect as to application and meaning, as "soluble cotton" for soluble nitro-cellulose; "insoluble cotton" for insoluble nitro-cellulose.

6.—Generic names for groups of varieties between which differences in chemical composition were recognized as existing; thus, nitro-celluloses as opposed to nitro-hydrocelluloses.

7.—Names referring to chemical composition as modified by extent and character of nitro-substitution, as "soluble nitro-cellulose of high nitration," of "low nitration."

DEFINITIONS

Cellulose.—The cell-wall or envelope of plant-tissues, to which the name *cellulose* has been applied as to a chemical individual. Unless the contrary is stated, the term cellulose, as employed in the present work, refers to pure cotton, unbleached and unspun, freed by mechanical treatment (ginning, picking, boiling, etc.) from wood, dirt, greases, resins, and foreign matter in general; either in the natural state, or as waste product from industrial processes.

Nitration.—The displacement of a number of atoms of replaceable hydrogen in cellulose, and the substitution therefor of the univalent radicle nitryl (NO_2). The term "nitration" is also employed to indicate the percentage of nitrogen in a given nitro-cellulose.

Nitro-cellulose.—Products resulting from the treatment of cellulose with strong nitric acid under the condition that they retain the cellular structure of the original cotton.

Nitro-cellulose of high nitration.—Those forms of nitro-cellulose in which a relatively large number of the replaceable hydrogen atoms are replaced by nitryl.

Nitro-cellulose of mean nitration.—Those forms of nitro-cellulose in which a mean number of the replaceable hydrogen atoms are replaced by nitryl.

Nitro-cellulose of low nitration.—Those forms of nitro-cellulose in which a relatively small number of replaceable hydrogen atoms are replaced by nitryl.

Insoluble nitro-cellulose.—Those forms of nitro-cellulose of high nitration insoluble at ordinary atmospheric temperatures in a mixture of two parts by weight of ethyl ether and one part by weight of ethyl alcohol.

Soluble nitro-cellulose.—Those forms of nitro-cellulose of low or mean nitration soluble at ordinary atmospheric temperature in a mixture of two parts by weight of ethyl ether and one part by weight of ethyl alcohol.

Hydrocellulose.—The product obtained by exposing cotton to the action of hydrochloric-acid fumes; or by immersing it in hydrochloric, dilute sulphuric, or very dilute nitric acid; a white pulverulent mass which, under the microscope, is seen to consist of fragments of the original fibre of modified cellular form.

Nitro-hydrocellulose.—Products resulting from the treatment of hydrocellulose with strong nitric acid under the condition that the resultant product retains the cellular structure originally possessed by the hydrocellulose.

Nitro-hydrocellulose of high nitration.—Those forms of nitro-hydrocellulose in which a relatively large number of the replaceable hydrogen atoms are replaced by nitryl.

Nitro-hydrocellulose of mean nitration. — Those forms of nitro-hydrocellulose in which a mean number of the replaceable hydrogen atoms are replaced by nitryl.

Nitro-hydrocellulose of low nitration.—Those forms of nitro-hydrocellulose in which a relatively small number of replaceable hydrogen atoms are replaced by nitryl.

Insoluble nitro-hydrocellulose.—Those forms of nitro-hydrocellulose of high nitration insoluble at ordinary atmospheric temperatures in a mixture of two parts by weight of ethyl ether and one part by weight of ethyl alcohol.

Soluble nitro-hydrocellulose.—Those forms of nitro-hydrocellulose of low or mean nitration soluble at ordinary atmospheric temperatures in a mixture of two parts by weight of ethyl ether and one part by weight of ethyl alcohol.

Gun-cotton.—The military name for those forms of highly explosive nitro-celluloses employed in war, and which are generally mixtures of a large quantity of insoluble with a small quantity of soluble nitro-cellulose and a very small quantity of unnitrated cotton.

Pyrocellulose.—Soluble nitro-cellulose of high *uniform* nitration, possessing a sufficient content of oxygen to convert its carbon into carbonic oxide and its hydrogen into aqueous vapor.

These terms, as defined above, will be employed so far as possible in the body of this treatise. The following list of synonyms is supplied for reference:

TABLE I

Name	Synonym
Nitro-cellulose,	Pyroxyline or pyroxylin.
Insoluble nitro-cellulose,	Insoluble gun-cotton ; insoluble cotton.
Soluble nitro-cellulose,	Soluble gun-cotton; soluble cotton; collodion-cotton; collodion-pyroxylin.
Soluble nitro-cellulose of low nitration.	Friable cotton.

CHAPTER II

EARLIER VIEWS AS TO NITRO-CELLULOSE COMPOSITION AND CONSTITUTION

EXISTING knowledge of the composition and constitution of nitro-cellulose still remains in a state of great confusion. A number of papers, scattered throughout the literature of experimental chemistry, and which throw valuable light upon the subject, have been published by independent investigators, while from time to time more elaborate articles summarizing the results of early workers have appeared. At least one excellent treatise upon cellulose has been published, * but it devotes only a few pages to the consideration of the nitro-celluloses. The reason for the existing confusion is that as yet no definite chemical structure has been determined for nitro-celluloses; they are regarded as nitro-substitution compounds, as ethers, or else their composition is considered as still doubtful.

If, however, the various original experimental results and the conclusions that have been drawn therefrom be examined in sequence, it will be observed that there does exist a *tendency* to account for the composition of these bodies on a definite hypothesis. There-

---

* "Cellulose," Cross and Bevan. London: Longmans, Green & Co., 1895.

fore the writer, in his endeavor to throw some light upon ultimate cellulose- and nitro-cellulose composition, will take up for consideration, first of all, in natural order of succession, results obtained by a number of students, each of whom, in his work, has supplied material from which subsequent investigators have drawn important conclusions.

Almost from the beginning of the study of the body the existence of more than one form was recognized. Domonte and Ménard's discovery that pyroxylin of low nitration was soluble in ether-alcohol, while the more highly nitrated variety remained insoluble therein; furnished a positive differentiation of nitro-celluloses into two groups; Béchamp showed that there existed nitro-celluloses of different nitrations soluble in ether-alcohol; and the only way of explaining the existence of such differences, in accordance with chemical theory, was by assuming that the substances of varying degrees of nitration obtained consisted of mixtures of various quantities of different, definite, chemical compounds.

The numerous attempts to explain both the mode of formation of nitro-cellulose as well as its constitution, and to reconcile results from its analyses, are well illustrated by the formulæ selected by early investigators to represent its varieties. Of these formulas, numerous series exist, extending from the original formula of Schönbein, through the later formulated, so-called mono-, di-, and trinitro-celluloses, to the series of six nitrates of Eder. At an early date the belief became established, based in all probability upon analogies furnished by the nitro-glycerins and nitro-benzols, that nitro-celluloses were mixtures of nitro-substitution products, which, assuming the composition of cellulose as $C_6H_{10}O_5$, were formulated as the tri-, di-, and mononitrates, with compositions $C_6H_7O_5(NO_2)_3$, $C_6H_8O_5(NO_2)_2$, and $C_6H_9O_5(NO_2)$, respectively. Of these, trinitro-cellulose was considered as identical with the insoluble variety of high nitration, and di-nitro-cellulose with that soluble in ether-alcohol; the existence of the mononitro-cellulose was predicated. Certain reactions due to these bodies led to a change of views concerning their chemical structure. Béchamp found that nitro-celluloses dissolved in ether-alcohol surrendered nitric acid upon addition of potash or ammonia, with the resultant formation of nitro-celluloses of lower nitration; he claimed for them the composition of ethers.*

Other reactions of the nitro-celluloses tend to supplement this view of their composition; e.g., ferric chloride and potassium and ammonium sulphydrates

---

* An ether is one of a class of organic bodies divided into two groups (1) simple ethers, consisting of two basic hydrocarbon radicles united by oxygen, and corresponding in constitution to the metallic oxides, as CH_3OCH_3, methyl ether, or methyl oxide, analogous to AgOAg, silver oxide ; (2) compound ethers, consisting of one or more basic or alcohol radicles and one or more acid or hydrocarbon radicles united by oxygen, and corresponding to the salts of the metals, as $CH_3COOC_2H_5$, ethyl acetate or acetic ether, corresponding to CH_3COONa, sodium acetate. Thus, if a cellulose be represented as possessing a composition $C_6H_{10}O_5$, and be written as a tribasic alcohol, $C_6H_7O_2(OH)_3$, then, on substituting nitryl, NO_2, for the replaceable hydrogen, we obtain $C_6H_7O_2O_3(NO_2)_3$, a compound nitric ether.

(Hadow, von Pettenkofer, cited by Guttmann) occasion the recovery of their cellulose, while the liberated nitric acid oxidizes the iron of the ferric chloride and transforms the sulphydrates into nitrates.

In 1878 Dr. J. M. Eder conducted a series of investigations into the character and composition of the nitro celluloses which has had much influence upon subsequent formation of thought in relation to the character and composition of these bodies; and from the results of his labors he was led to conclude that there existed no less than six distinct varieties of them, three of which, the hexa-, penta-, and di-, he was able to isolate; two of them, the tetra- and tri-, he obtained in admixture; the mononitro-cellulose, however, he was unable to prepare. Doubling the coefficients of cellulose to avoid fractional coefficients in the derivatives, he formulated his series of nitrates as follows:

TABLE II

Name	Composition
Cellulose hexanitrate	$C_{12}H_{14}O_4(NO_3)_6$
Cellulose pentanitrate	$C_{12}H_{15}O_5(NO_3)_5$
Cellulose tetranitrate	$C_{12}H_{16}O_6(NO_3)_4$
Cellulose trinitrate	$C_{12}H_{17}O_7(NO_3)_3$
Cellulose dinitrate	$C_{12}H_{18}O_8(NO_3)_2$
Cellulose mononitrate	——

Dr. Eder's work constituted a purely scientific research into the chemical properties of a group of bodies. Subsequent investigations are characterized by the partial subordination of their scientific aims to the demands of the useful arts. These investigations are of two kinds, and refer to the technical uses of the soluble and insoluble varieties respectively. Those upon the soluble nitro-celluloses relate, for example, to photography,—to questions of transparency and uniformity of thickness of film; those upon insoluble nitro-celluloses, to the art of war and to the attainment of the highest explosive effect consistent with the maintenance of stability. The general purpose of the present work is the study of the physical and chemical properties of nitro-celluloses and nitro-cellulose colloids, their methods of preparation, and their explosive qualities; and to the prosecution of this study investigations of the second class have, until recently, afforded the more direct aid. Conditions of research have, however, been recently modified. For, whereas the explosives prepared from cotton were formerly insoluble nitro-celluloses (gun-cottons) susceptible of detonation as well as of combustion, and employed in mines and torpedoes, yet in recent times the field of research has been extended to the soluble varieties in the effort to secure a suitable base material for the preparation of a non-detonating, progressively-burning, smokeless powder.

The following account of Eder's nitrates (taken from Cross and Bevan, "Cellulose" *) may be quoted here:

"Hexanitrate, $C_{12}H_{14}O_4(NO_3)_6$, gun-cotton. In the formation of this body, nitric acid of 1.5 sp. gr. and sulphuric acid of 1.84 sp. gr. are mixed in varying proportions, about 3 of nitric to 1 of sulphuric; sometimes this proportion is reversed, and cotton

---

immersed in this at a temperature not exceeding 10° C. for 24 hours; 100 parts of cellulose yield about 175 of cellulose nitrate. The hexanitrate so prepared is insoluble in alcohol, ether, or mixtures of both, in glacial acetic acid or methyl alcohol. Acetone dissolves it very slowly. This is the most explosive gun-cotton. It ignites at 160°–170° C. According to Eder the mixtures of nitre and sulphuric acid do not give this nitrate. Ordinary gun-cotton may contain as much as 12 per cent. of nitrates soluble in ether-alcohol. The hexanitrate seems to be the only one quite insoluble in ether-alcohol."

"Pentanitrate, $C_{12}H_{15}O_6(NO_3)_5$. This composition has been very commonly ascribed to gun-cotton. It is difficult, if not impossible, to prepare it in a state of purity by the direct action of acid on cellulose. The best method is the one devised by Eder, making use of the property discovered by De Vrij, that gun-cotton (hexanitrate) dissolves in nitric acid at about 80° or 90° C., and is precipitated, as the pentanitrate, by concentrated sulphuric acid after cooling to 0° C.; after mixing with a large volume of water, and washing the precipitate with water and then with alcohol, it is dissolved in ether-alcohol and again precipitated with water, when it is obtained pure. This nitrate is insoluble in alcohol, but dissolves readily in ether-alcohol, and slightly in acetic acid. Strong potassa solution converts this nitrate into the dinitrate, $C_{12}H_{18}O_8(NO_3)_2$."

"The tetra- and trinitrates (collodion-pyroxylin) are generally formed together when cellulose is treated with a more dilute nitric acid, and at a higher temperature, and for a much shorter time (13–20 minutes), than in the formation of the hexanitrate. It is not possible to separate them, as they are soluble to the same extent in ether-alcohol, acetic ether, acetic acid, or wood-spirit. On treatment with concentrated nitric and sulphuric acids, both the tri- and tetranitrates are converted into pentanitrate and hexanitrate. Potassa and ammonia convert them into dinitrate.''

''Cellulose dinitrate, $C_{12}H_{18}O_8(NO_2)_2$, is formed by the action of alkalies on the other nitrates, and also by the action of hot dilute nitric acid on cellulose. The dinitrate is very soluble in alcohol-ether, acetic ether, and in absolute alcohol. Further action of alkalies on the dinitrate results in a complete decomposition of the molecule, some organic acids and tarry matters being formed.''

The next after Eder to increase our knowledge of the character and relationships of the members of the nitro-cellulose series was M. Vieille (Comptes Rendus, **95,** 132), the eminent French savant, whose efforts (in collaboration with M. Sarrau) were crowned with success in the production and establishment of the manufacture of a successful smokeless powder in France. M. Vieille's researches were published in part in the French official journal of explosives, the Mémorial des Poudres et Salpêtres,* a translation of

---

* ''Recherches sur la Nitrification du Coton,'' by M. Vieille, Ingénieur des Poudres et Salpêtres, Vol. II., 1889, Paris: Gauthiers-Villars et Fils.

the article referred to constituting Appendix I of the present work.

Vieille's method consisted in selecting acid mixtures of specified standard strengths, nitrating under regularly controlled conditions as to mass, time, and temperature, determining the nitration of the resultant products, and plotting upon diagrams the resultant nitrations as referred to the strengths of the acid mixtures used to produce them. In this manner he was enabled to recognize a tendency of nitration towards groupings or discontinuities, rather than towards progressively increasing nitration, advancing in measure with increase in strength of acids; and he interpreted this tendency as indicating the existence of a number of definite cellulose nitrates. He summarizes the results of his work as follows:

"In order to account completely for the different changes (groupings, discontinuities) by the production of nitro-products corresponding to definite formulæ, the equivalent of nitro-cellulose must be quadrupled. Nitro-celluloses corresponding to such formulæ agree with the theoretical yields of nitrogen dioxide per gram of material indicated in the following table, and which correspond either to the discontinuities to which we have alluded, or else to a change of physical properties."

While Dr. Eder formulated *six* varieties of nitrated material, doubling the coefficients of cellulose by writing it $C_{12}H_{20}O_{10}$, instead of $C_6H_{10}O_5$, M. Vieille formulates no less than *eight* compounds, to express which he quadruples coefficients, writing cellulosé as $C_{24}H_{40}O_{20}$. He thus obtains:

TABLE III

		Theoretical c.c. of NO_2	Experimental c.c. of NO_2
$C_{24}H_{30}O_{20}(NO_2)_{11}$	Cellulose endecanitrate, } gun-cottons	214	215
$C_{24}H_{30}O_{20}(NO_2)_{10}$	Cellulose decanitrate,	203	215
$C_{24}H_{31}O_{20}(NO_2)_9$	Cellulose enneanitrate, } collodions	100	192
$C_{24}H_{32}O_{20}(NO_2)_8$	Cellulose octonitrate,	178	182
$C_{24}H_{33}O_{20}(NO_2)_7$	Cellulose heptanitrate, } friable cottons	162	164
$C_{24}H_{34}O_{20}(NO_2)_6$	Cellulose hexanitrate,	146	143
$C_{24}H_{35}O_{20}(NO_2)_5$	Cellulose pentanitrate,	128	132
$C_{24}H_{36}O_{20}(NO_2)_4$	Cellulose tetranitrate	108	109

To illustrate the accordance of theory with practice, the content of nitrogen (dioxide), as it should
exist according to theory, is compared in each case
with that actually determined from practical experiment. From the above there would appear to be
two varieties of gun-cotton insoluble in ether-alcohol,
two varieties of soluble nitro-celluloses, and a number
of varieties of nitro-celluloses of lower nitration. M.
Vieille's paper was published shortly after the official
announcement by the French Government of the development and successful establishment of the manufacture of an efficient smokeless powder, these results
being the declared fruits of M. Vieille's researches,
and it is therefore authoritative.

The points to which attention are especially called
in M. Vieille's work are the quadrupling of the expo-
nents of cellulose, and the formulation of as many as
eight varieties of its nitro-derivatives.

The abandonment of the old types of smoke-form-
ing powders that had been in use for hundreds of
years, and the substitution therefor, by the French
government, of a new and efficient smokeless powder,
was a step that naturally attracted the attention of all
civilized powers. The composition of the French
powders and their methods of manufacture remained
carefully guarded secrets. Efforts to achieve similar
results were at once inaugurated in other countries,
and the period of inactivity following the abandonment of efforts to employ gun-cotton as a propellant
gave way to one of marked activity in all that related
to the study of explosives. Shortly after the an-

nouncement of the results obtained in France, the
Russian government commissioned Professor D. Mendeléef, a chemist who had already achieved world-
wide reputation as the expounder of the Periodic
Law of existence of the elements, to conduct a series
of researches with a view to the production of an
efficient smokeless powder for Russia. As the result
of his labors Professor Mendeléef succeeded in developing a powder called by him "pyrocollodion,"
which proved satisfactory, and which was adopted
in Russia for use in arms of all calibres. As in the
case of its predecessor in France, the composition and
method of manufacture of pyrocollodion remain care-
fully-guarded national secrets. Outlines of ballistic
results have been published, however, and it is by
these that the next light is thrown upon the composition of nitro-celluloses.

The scope of Professor Mendeléef's work, and the
character of the analytical methods followed by him,
may be ascertained from an examination of a paper
published by him, my translation of which constitutes
Appendix II of the present work. In relation to
the structure of the nitro-celluloses he states:

"In all aldehydes, beginning with the formic and
the acetic, a tendency towards polymerization is to be
noted, due, doubtless, to the property of aldehydes
of entering into various combinations (with H_2O,
$NaHSO_3$, etc.); whence the composition $C_6H_{10}O_5$,
containing an aldehyde grouping, should also possess
this property, so far as relates thereto. We may
therefore safely assume that the molecular composi-

tion of cellulose, judging from its properties, is polymerized, i.e., it is of the form $C_{6n}H_{10n}O_{6n}$, where n is probably very great."

It will be seen from the foregoing that in their efforts to explain the atomic constitution of nitro-cellulose, investigators have invariably been led to increase the common multiple of the elements entering into the composition of cellulose, until finally Mendeléef states as his opinion that this multiple may be very great through reason of the presence of certain tendencies towards polymerization. It is interesting to observe how different chemists have been led to establish conclusions as to the existence of compounds corresponding to the formulæ they have written. Eder dissolves out of gun-cotton its soluble content, and as the result of the analysis of the remaining portion writes its formula as double tri-, or hexanitro-cellulose, $C_{12}H_{14}(NO_2)_6O_{10}$; he isolates from cotton treated with weaker acids, a compound corresponding in content of nitrogen to what a body of constitution $C_{12}H_{15}(NO_2)_5O_{10}$, a pentanitro-cellulose, should give, and obtains through the agency of solution a nitro-cellulose precipitate satisfying the desired conditions. He also obtains, by employing acids of still further reduced strengths, a body of variable composition which he regards as a mixture of tetra- and trinitro-celluloses, but does not succeed in isolating the two distinct bodies from the mixture. Vieille employs mixtures of acids increasing in strength progressively; continues the process of nitration through a period of time sufficiently long to insure the total conversion of the cellulose into nitro-cellulose (as shown by the employment of a solution of iodine in potassium iodide as an indicator of free cellulose); refers to coördinate axes the results of each observation, employing strengths of acids as abscissæ, and numbers of cubic centimetres of nitric oxide evolved as ordinates. Upon comparing results he notes a tendency towards the existence of progressive steps in nitration; i.e., for an acid varying somewhat above and below a certain point in strength there appears to be formed a definite product of nitration. Taking into account the number of such steps observed and their distances apart, he formulates the series of compounds enumerated in a preceding paragraph.

CHAPTER III

THE CONCEPTION OF PROGRESSION IN RELATION TO COMPOSITION AND CONSTITUTION

CELLULOSE is distinguishable from other materials employed for purposes of nitration by the possession of a *continuous*, complex, and definite cell structure. The plant producing it has developed by growth from the protoplasmic state, through influences of soil, atmosphere, and sunlight; after its death the cellulose tissues remain, the skeleton of the once living organism, possessing a structure bestowed by successive growth processes and not by any definite and general chemical change occurring at any stated time. It is this remaining tissue, an organization of cells infinite in their variety and form, that constitutes the base material employed for nitration. We may proceed to nitrate it in various ways; we may first partially destroy or disintegrate the cell structure (convert it into hydrocellulose); the nitration may be conducted at various temperatures and continued for different lengths of time with the employment of various acid mixtures of different strengths, and with the use of different relative quantities of cotton and acids. If all of these governing conditions be taken account of, and if proper allowance be made for their effect, we may predicate for the nitrated product an exact composition and exact qualities; if any of them be overlooked, we lose control of physical character and chemical composition of the final product.

The method of accounting for the composition of nitro-cellulose by assuming it to consist of a mixture of the different members of a graded series of cellulose nitrates—themselves definite chemical compounds— was a rational procedure in accordance with established chemical usage; yet there existed grave difficulties in the way of maintaining such views. In the first place, the members of the series could not be separated from one another. Eder was unable to separate cellulose tetra- and trinitrates. The impossibility of resolving a given nitro-cellulose into definite quantities of the various compounds formulated by Vieille, Eder, or their predecessors, is generally recognized by every investigator to-day. In the second place, the conception of a definite period of time being required to effect nitration is inseparably connected with the formation of these bodies. Thus properly nitrated gun-cotton consists of a large quantity of insoluble with a small quantity of soluble and a very small quantity of unnitrated cotton; but if nitration be arrested before completion, there results a mixture of different quantities of nitrated and unnitrated cotton.

That the nitration of cellulose is a gradual progressive process, advancing from incipiency through lapse of time towards completion, was the next theory advanced. This change in treatment of the problem, which virtually led to the abandonment of the old simple formulation advocated, is discussed with great clearness by M. Bruley, a French Government chemist, in a paper entitled " Sur la Fabrication des Cotons Nitrés," published in the Mémorial des Poudres et Salpêtres (Vol. VIII, 1895–6), my translation of which constitutes Apendix III of the present work.

For purposes of elucidation, Bruley's work will be considered comparatively, in relation to what has been accomplished by others. The first investigators treated cellulose with nitric acid direct, and obtained a product to which they endeavored to ascribe a formula; their successors demonstrated the existence of more than one variety of nitro-cellulose, and formulated a series of compounds. The various acid mixtures employed in these researches may be divided into two classes: those composed of nitric acid and water taken in various proportions, and those containing sulphuric acid in addition to nitric acid and water. It was understood how the absorptive action of the sulphuric acid rendered possible the formation of cellulose nitrates of higher nitration than those that could be obtained by the employment of concentrated nitric acid alone. But mixtures of concentrated nitric and sulphuric acids necessarily contain water, anhydrous sulphuric acid being a solid and anhydrous nitric acid being impossible to prepare; while with the more highly diluted mixture of the two acids cellulose nitrates identical with those formed with nitric acid and water alone could be formed; therefore the widest range of nitration resulted from the employment of mixtures containing nitric and sulphuric acids and water.

Vieille had already studied the nitro-products formed by the use of mixtures containing various proportionate quantities of nitric and sulphuric acids of definite strengths. Bruley's investigations covered the broader field resulting from the employment of mixtures of the three elements, in which the quantity present of each element varied *in all practicable proportions* in reference to the quantities of the other two. The scope of the latter work may be graphically indicated as follows:

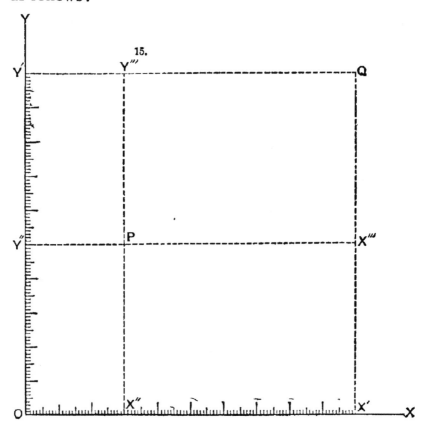

Let OX and OY be coördinate axes. On OY lay off OY', which divide into one hundred equal parts; and let OY'' represent the number of parts of nitric acid to one hundred parts of sulphuric acid. Then $Y''X'''$, parallel to OX, will be the locus of all points corresponding to mixtures in which the amounts of nitric and sulphuric acids present bear the definite ratio $\dfrac{OY''}{OY'}$ to each other. On OX lay off OX' and divide it into one hundred equal parts, and let OX'' represent the number of parts of water to one hundred parts of sulphuric acid. Then $X''Y'''$, parallel to OY, will be the locus of all points corresponding to mixtures in which the quantities of water and sulphuric acid present bear the definite ratio $\dfrac{OX''}{OY'}$ to one another.

The point P, in which the lines $Y''X'''$ and $X''Y'''$ intersect, corresponds to a mixture containing definite quantities of nitric acid, sulphuric acid, and water. The area $OY'OX'$ is a rectangle, every point of which corresponds to some one combination of the three elements. M. Bruley explores this area by choosing a number of approximately equidistant points distributed over its surface, preparing the acid mixtures corresponding to them, and determining the nitration and solubility of the nitro-celluloses prepared from these mixtures. Proceeding in this manner, and joining points of equal nitration, he maps out a series of parallel or nearly parallel curves, between which are included areas of equal or similar solubility. The following diagram, taken from M. Bruley's work, illustrates the method:

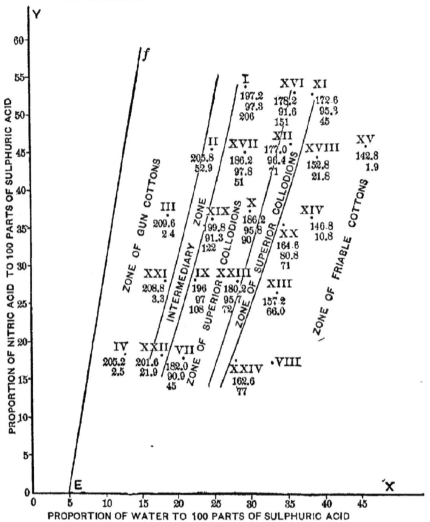

The Roman numeral is the serial number of experiment; the upper Arabic numeral, the nitration in cubic centimetres of NO_2, the second, the solubility; and the third, when given, the viscosity.

The nearer the points corresponding to nitrations lie to the line Ef, which is the locus of mixtures containing the least possible quantities of water, the higher the nitrations. The area is divided into belts corresponding to mixtures forming insoluble nitro-celluloses, "intermediate" nitro-celluloses, collodions of higher and of lower nitration, and "friable" cottons. The published investigations do not consider mixtures containing more than 55 parts of nitric to 100 parts of sulphuric acid, M. Bruley stating that mixtures containing more than this relative proportion of nitric acid are "not practicable commercially from their increased cost"; nor those containing less than 15 parts of nitric to 100 parts of the sulphuric acid present; in these nitration proceeds with exceeding slowness. Similarly, mixtures containing less than 35 per cent. of water, compared with the quantity of sulphuric acid present, embrace all those capable of producing nitrations higher than those of "friable" cottons; while the lower limit of water is fixed by the strength of the strongest acids commercially obtainable.

Besides nitration and solubility, a new characteristic of the nitrated product is here introduced,—viscosity, —as determined by the rate of flow, in drops per minute, through a standard orifice, of a standard solution of the collodion under examination. M. Bruley states that increased temperature of nitration, as well as continued pulping and washing in warm water, all have the effect of diminishing the viscosity of the collodions formed from nitro-cellulose; but he does not discuss the practical bearing of this fact on the manufacture of colloids.

M. Bruley also discusses briefly relations of time

and temperature to nitration.   The duration of the reaction is found to be the more prolonged the smaller the quantity of nitric acid present in the nitrating mixture; an immersion of two hours is found to suffice, in general, for the production of the soluble nitrocelluloses; but as much as eight to ten hours are required to complete the nitration of gun-cotton.   A comparison is made of nitrations conducted at three different temperatures, employing the same acids and cotton;   and the conclusion is reached that, in the case of soluble nitro-celluloses, increase of temperature during dipping and reaction increases ultimate nitration and solubility; while for gun-cotton, though the effect of temperature upon solubility is less distinctly marked, yet high temperatures have the effect of increasing solubilities.

During the years 1895 and 1896, I conducted series of experiments at the Naval Torpedo Station, at Newport, Rhode Island, with the view to the production of a nitro-cellulose base suitable for conversion, by direct colloidization, into an efficient smokeless powder.*   The problem presented itself in the form of an attempt to transform well-known types of nitro-celluloses, with or without the addition of solid, non-colloidable ingredients, and by the use of standard solvents, into colloid powders; and it ultimately resolved into an effort to overcome certain ballistic inconveniences, the existence of which was not recognized when the experiments were begun.   In the endeavor to over-

---

* I have continued experimenting in this field, at intervals, ever since this time.—J. B. B.

come these inconveniences, it became apparent that
there was little hope of preparing from the old materials a powder capable of fulfilling service requirements; and the results, wholly negative, of elaborate
and exhaustive series of experiments with the old
materials, forced me to the conclusion that, if a suitable powder were developed, it could only be through
the discovery of a new form of nitro-cellulose capable
of colloidization, and which would possess physical
and chemical properties not pertaining to any hitherto
existing known form of this substance.

As the result of my labors I succeeded in developing such a new form of nitro-cellulose, which I was
able to convert directly, by colloidization, without
addition of other ingredient, into a colloid smokeless
powder, suitable for arms of all calibres. With this
powder I conducted extended series of experiments,
testing and establishing its keeping qualities, and stand-
ardizing weights of charge and dimensions of grain for
the different calibres of guns. Its manufacture was
established on a commercial scale at the Torpedo Station, at Newport, Rhode Island, where the represen-
tatives of the various private powder-manufacturing
establishments were instructed in the method of preparation of the new material.* Subsequently these firms
established plants of their own on a scale far larger

---

* At this time (1894–1897) the Naval Torpedo Station, at Newport, Rhode Island, was under the command of Captain George
A. Converse, U. S. Navy, to whose ability as an administrator,
as well as mechanical skill as a specialist, the successful development of smokeless powder is largely attributable.

than that undertaken at Newport; and finally an appropriation was secured for the Navy, sufficient for the erection of a plant large enough to enable this branch of the service to manufacture an appreciable share of the powder consumed afloat.

The steps leading up to the development of the new nitro-cellulose are cited here in relation to the light they throw upon ultimate cellulose and nitrocellulose structure. Taken in order of approximate sequence they may be outlined as follows:

1.—Powders were prepared by colloiding insoluble, soluble, and mixtures of insoluble and soluble nitrocelluloses in acetone (both varieties of nitro-cellulose readily colloid in this solvent), forming the resultant material into strips of different thicknesses, firing charges of different' weights of each thickness from standard guns, and tabulating resultant velocities and pressures. Besides the pure colloids thus obtained there were experimented with other colloids having incorporated into them various percentages of barium and potassium nitrates, both deposited from solution and employed in the dry pulverulent state. It was observed that the addition of the nitrates led to the development of smoke, but increased the value of V/P, the ratio of the maximum pressure to the initial velocity realized.

2.—A large quantity of gun-cotton, then stored at the Torpedo Station, was available for conversion into powder. It was found that different manufactured lots of this material produced powders differing widely in ballistic properties. To determine the cause of these differences, I took blocks of each gun-cotton in store (some fifty odd lots), washed, dried, and sifted each sample,—the washing to remove the sodium carbonate,—colloided each with the same acetone, formed the resultant masses into small rectangular grains of the same dimensions and dried them. I then placed one·gram weights of each small lot upon slips of glass and ignited them in the open. The ashes remaining after combustion differed very greatly among themselves, some assuming the form of a fine white residue, others of a sooty mass of unconsumed carbon. Upon comparing the ash residues with the results of the complete chemical analyses of the original cottons subsequently made, I found that, for the cases where carbon was deposited, the gun-cottons from which the powder had been made contained an abnormally large quantity of free unnitrated cotton, the existence of which had not hitherto been suspected.

3.—Those lots of gun-cotton containing large quantities of free unnitrated cotton being eliminated, experiments with powders prepared from the remaining lots were continued. Ballistic differences were still found to obtain, although less marked than those primarily observed. Upon comparing the nitration of the original gun-cottons,—which differed among themselves considerably, ranging between $N = 13.4$ and $N = 12.4$,— with the ballistic results from the powders prepared from them, it was found that the brusquer powders, which developed high pressures as corresponding to comparatively low velocities, were prepared from gun-cottons of highest nitration. It occurred to me, therefore, that uniformity in ballistic conditions might be preserved through the maintenance of mean nitration, i.e , by blending different lots of nitro-celluloses together, so that the mean nitrogen contents of all blends should be maintained a constant; at the same time providing that dimensions of powder-grains and weights of charge remained equal. The truth of this theoretical assumption was abundantly sustained by the results of practical experiment, and the problem of the attainment of ballistic uniformity, using gun-cotton and the old forms of soluble nitro-celluloses as basis materials for the manufacture of colloid powder, was solved. Bearing in mind the actual nitrations of the various lots of gun-cottons on hand, I chose a mean of 12.75 per cent. N as a standard of nitration, and blended the successive lots to this figure, adding soluble nitro-cellulose when it became necessary to reduce lots of especially high nitration down to the standard.

4.—I observed, as the result of experiment, that the velocity corresponding to a given bore-pressure could be increased by incorporating oxygen-carriers, such as barium and potassium nitrates, in certain percentages into colloid powders; and to such an extent that for a pressure of fifteen tons a gain of about 300 foot-seconds could be realized. I attributed this difference in ballistic effect to an accelerative action due to the oxidation of the products of combustion of the nitro-cellulose *after* their evolution in the bore of the gun and before leaving the gun, by the gaseous oxides of

nitrogen evolved from the metallic nitrates.* As the
bodies to which accelerative effect was attributable
were free, inert particles distributed throughout the
substance of the colloid, I argued that free, uncolloided gun-cotton distributed throughout an ether-
alcohol colloid of soluble nitro-cellulose would produce
the same effect. Experiments with free gun-cotton as
an " accelerator " proved failures, however, practically
no ballistic difference being observed between the action of the ether-alcohol colloid of the soluble, containing free insoluble nitro-cellulose and certain other colloids of the same in which both ingredients were present
in the colloid state. The fact was that both the soluble and insoluble forms of nitro-cellulose were, in
both cases, *consumed away at practically the same rate.*

5.—The effort to prepare powders from colloided
soluble nitro-celluloses into which uncolloided insoluble
nitro-cellulose was incorporated as an accelerator, led
to extended series of experiments with ether-alcohol
colloids. These proved at first difficult to manufacture,
but, once prepared, were found manifestly superior to
the acetone colloids, as they were extremely tough
and well capable of resisting disintegration in the gun
at the instant of firing,—in which regard the brittle
acetone colloids had not proved altogether satisfactory. Actual experiments in firing had also shown
that the greater the quantity of uncolloided (insoluble)

---

* See Appendix IV, which is a reprint of my paper entitled
" Development of Smokeless Powder," published in the Proceed-
ings of the U. S. Naval Inst., in which the subject of acceleration
is treated at some length.

nitro-cellulose present in an ether-alcohol colloid powder, the brusquer the powder proved, developing a higher bore-pressure as corresponding to the muzzle velocity realized. But, in order to maintain a standard nitration,—explosive strength,—it was necessary to have present always a considerable quantity of the un-colloided (insoluble) form of nitro-cellulose. As this was objectionable for the above reason, I therefore began experimenting, to see how far the nitration of the soluble nitro-cellulose could be raised,—with the view of minimizing the amount of insoluble nitro-cellulose that would be required

6.—I also made investigations in another line, and conducted firing trials with a series of powders prepared from nitro-hydrocelluloses. A note upon the constitution of this body may be pertinent here.

When cotton is exposed to the action of hydrochloric acid, in the form of gas or of concentrated aqueous solution, it undergoes a change of form and composition, being converted into a material known as hydrocellulose, the composition of which has been variously regarded. Viewed as a substitution product, it is formulated as a cellulose hydrate (Girard, cited by Cross and Bevan); considered physically, it appears to consist of an aggregation of fragments of the cells from which the original cellulose was built up. The fibres seem attacked along planes where their sub-stance is most readily susceptible of decomposition by the acid and are separated from one another; the action of the acid appears to be a cutting of cell-joints over planes of weakness, whereby the fibres are divided into small lengths which are clearly visible under the microscope. (There would thus seem to be some portions of the cell more readily susceptible to attack than other portions.) If the process be incomplete, partial separation only occurs, long unattacked fibres remaining in quantity.

Samples of nitro-hydrocellulose, wholly soluble in ether-alcohol, of nitration as high as 12.6 to 12.7 per cent., were obtained by nitrating hydrocellulose in the acid mixtures I was employing to prepare directly mixtures of insoluble and soluble nitro-cellulose from cotton. This led to extended series of trials of powders, of both the accelerated and the unaccelerated types, containing different quantities of the two varieties of nitro-hydrocelluloses in various proportions, with a view of investigating their stability and their ballistic properties.

On account of their extreme brittleness, these colloid powders proved too brusque, and experiments with them were abandoned. They also failed in certain cases to develop normal stability.

7.—The observation of certain remarkable phenomena connected with the effect of decrease in temperature in promoting the solution and colloidization of certain forms of nitro-cellulose in certain solvents,—to which reference is made in detail in a subsequent portion of this work,—led me to take up the consideration of *temperature*, as an important factor in the control of the character and degree of nitration. I conducted extended series of experiments in which cotton was nitrated in various acid mixtures at temperatures ranging between 0° C. and 80° C. The result of these experiments was the development of pyrocellulose,—a form of soluble nitro-cellulose of high nitration, which, for a given weight of its substance, converted into colloid grains of standard dimensions and dried, developed, when fired from the standard gun, the highest muzzle velocity, as compared with a given limiting bore pressure.

The results of the observations in this regard may be briefly summarized as follows:

The physical and chemical, characteristics of products of nitration are subject to radical modifications, through variation of temperature at which the reaction is conducted. Increase of temperature has the effect of raising the nitration of both the soluble and the insoluble varieties, and would appear also to increase the percentage of the soluble component in a blend of the soluble and insoluble varieties. The heat employed may be derived from two sources: (1) that evolved during the exothermic reaction of the nitration of cellulose; (2) that which is supplied from external sources to additionally raise the temperature of the nitrating mass. If the temperature of the nitrating mass be raised above a certain point, the structure of the cellulose is attacked, and the nitro-celluloses cease to form, the material dissolving in the acid, with the resultant formation of nitro-substitution bodies of other genera, such as the nitro-saccharoses; or else, direct decomposition of the nitrated body ensues, with evolution of copious fumes of nitric-oxide gas.

The chemical and physical phenomena attending

both the decomposition and formation of nitro-celluloses are largely controlled by temperature. Thus,
the explosive force of gun-cotton is greatly reduced
by freezing the latter. Gun-cotton saturated with
liquid air is not only not an explosive, but is practically
a non-combustible; while non-nitrated cotton under
similar conditions is a violent explosive.*

Again, as will be shown hereafter, the extent of solubility of certain nitro-celluloses in certain solvents is
a function of the temperature at which the solution is
undertaken; so that the relative quantities of the
soluble and insoluble constituents in a mixture of
nitro-celluloses formed at one operation may depend
upon the temperature at which the separation of the
sub-constituents is effected.

---

* The result of experiments made by me in New York in Octo-
ber, 1899.

CHAPTER IV

SOLUTIONS OF NITRO-CELLULOSE. THEORY OF THE CELLULOSE MOLECULE

CELLULOSE is found to possess, after nitration, a remarkable property that unnitrated cellulose does not possess: it dissolves freely in a number of liquids, in which it is not soluble in the unnitrated state. Of these, the solvents ethyl ether, ethyl alcohol, ether-alcohol, and acetone are of special interest, both from their connection with the manufacture of smokeless powder, and from the physical and chemical bearings of their methods of effecting solutions. From the solutions the nitro-cellulose forms with them it may be precipitated by the addition of an excess of water or other liquid in which it is not soluble, in a flocculent form; and ultimately, after drying, forms a pulverulent mass. It is to be specially remarked that the nitro-cellulose cannot be recovered in its original cellular state; the process of solution has destroyed its organic structure, which may not be recovered or recreated.

The process of effecting the solution of the nitro-cellulose may be regarded as preliminary to the formation of the colloid. All forms of nitro-cellulose dissolve freely in an excess of those solvents, in contact with smaller quantities of which they form colloids directly. If the quantity of solvent be reduced below a certain point in proportion to the quantity of nitro-cellulose employed, colloidization ensues without previous liquefaction; if the solvent be sufficient in quantity to effect liquefaction, evaporation of excess of solvent must precede colloidization; if the one state can be produced, the possibility of forming the other may be predicated.

The line between solution and colloidization is not to be drawn sharply; the two states of matter merging into one another. There are, however, two distinct sets of progressive steps or series of physical changes. to be observed, through one or the other of which these bodies pass in their transformation from the liquid to the solid state, and which may be expressed with reference to their progression as follows:

First series: (*a*) liquid; (*b*) jelly; (*c*) elastic mass; (*d*) tough colloid.

Second series: (*a*) liquid; (*b*) slime; (*c*) plastic mass; (*d*) brittle colloid.

To Series I belong most ether-alcohol colloids; to Series II, most acetone colloids.

The purpose of the present chapter is to describe nitro-cellulose solutions, the methods of forming them, and their characteristics apart from consideration of their colloidal evaporated residues; and to present in relation thereto certain theoretical considerations throwing light upon the chemical constitution of cellulose and its nitrates. The subjects of colloids, their properties and methods of formation, will be treated subsequently.

A discussion of the solubility of nitro-celluloses may best be prefaced by an account of a remarkable property of soluble nitro-celluloses in general, especially characteristic of pyrocellulose and of those forms of nitro-hydrocellulose soluble in ether-alcohol; viz., the direct solubility of these bodies in the solvent ether * when subjected to the influence of cold.

In August, 1896, I conducted a series of experiments with soluble nitro-hydrocellulose of very high nitration, to determine its adaptability for conversion into smokeless powder; this material, colloided in ether-alcohol and dried, had given promise of value as a progressive explosive.

Upon a very warm Sunday afternoon, I visited a dry-house in which a small tray of soluble nitro-hydrocellulose, of high nitration (N 12.4+), was exposed to a moderate drying temperature. Removing about one gram of the amorphous gray powder from the drying-tray, I introduced it into a test-tube, which I tightly closed with a rubber stopper to prevent the absorption of moisture. I then visited the chemical laboratory and partly filled the tube with what I supposed to be ether-alcohol. To my disappointment the precipitate did not dissolve. Upon agitation, it diffused itself throughout the liquid, but rapidly settled to the bottom, in its original pulverulent form, when brought to rest. I at first attributed this behavior to excessive nitration, believing the material to con-

---

*When "ether" and "alcohol" are referred to without qualification, they are intended to designate ethyl ether and ethyl alcohol.

sist of insoluble instead of soluble nitro cellulose. Having observed, however, during the previous winter that certain of the insoluble nitro-hydrocelluloses appeared to exhibit a tendency to enter into solution upon exposure to cold (a portion of the precipitate appearing to rise in the tube, like a jelly, under the influence of cold), it occurred to me to try the effect of a salt-and-ice freezing mixture upon the tube and its contents. I therefore mixed a small quantity of salt and ice in a beaker, into which I introduced the tube in a central vertical position. To my great satisfaction, the whole of the precipitate went rapidly into solution, forming a yellowish-brown, mobile fluid.

While considering the phenomenon that I had witnessed, I remained seated at my desk, holding the test-tube enclosed within the palm of my hand. Suddenly I noticed that, although I had shifted the tube into the inverted position (cork downwards), yet the contents, masked by my hand, had not observed the law of liquid flow, for the lower uncovered end of the test-tube, which extended downwards, was empty. Carefully opening my hand, I was surprised to find that the contents of the tube had condensed into a dense jelly, which remained fixed in the upper part of the tube. I re-introduced the tube into the freezing mixture; its contents liquefied as before, being transformed into a liquid as mobile as maple-syrup; removal from the source of cold and immersion in water heated to about 100° F. (38° C.), or holding in the palm of the hand, sufficed to cause the liquid to congeal.

The phenomenon above described related to the behavior of soluble nitro-hydrocellulose in the presence of an excess of solvent (ether) when contained in a sealed vessel which is exposed successively to different temperatures; removal of the cork with subsequent evaporation of the solvent results in the formation of a solid colloid residue, non-liquefiable upon variation of temperature.

After producing the results above described, I next endeavored to duplicate them. To my surprise, the soluble nitro-cellulose, which I supposed the same as that I employed the day before, promptly went into solution in ether-alcohol at a temperature of about 70° F. Investigation led to the discovery of an unfortunate interchange of trays in the dry-house, which rendered it impossible to repeat with certainty the experiment cited. There was, therefore, but one mode of procedure left—to select sample lots from all the trays, one of which must represent the lot originally taken, and experiment with them in the presence of ether-alcohol. Still I was unable to obtain the original results. It next occurred to me that I might have employed by mistake some solvent other than ether-alcohol, and as the result of a day's experimenting, I found that phenomena identical with those originally developed could be obtained with soluble nitro-hydrocelluloses using ethyl ether as a solvent.

Experimenting subsequently, 1899–1900, to ascertain whether the above phenomena were peculiar to nitro-hydrocelluloses, or whether they were characteristic of all soluble nitro-celluloses, I found:

1.—That pyrocellulose could be readily dissolved in ether upon application of cold.

2.—That all soluble nitro-celluloses acted similarly in presence of an excess of ether, but that some were more readily disintegrated by ether upon application of cold than others.

3.—That if the necessary degree of cold were developed, soluble nitro-celluloses were not only soluble to any desired extent in ether, but that they could be colloided directly therein, without recourse to liquefaction.

4.—That the addition of a few drops of alcohol in difficult cases appeared to be equivalent to a lowering of temperature, i.e., it rendered a given soluble nitro-cellulose more soluble in ether, in the presence of a given degree of cold, than it otherwise would have been.

The problem of nitro-cellulose solution may be appropriately prefaced with the query: Why are certain forms of soluble nitro-cellulose readily soluble at ordinary atmospheric temperatures in a compound of two parts by weight of ethyl ether with one part by weight of ethyl alcohol; whereas, the said forms of nitro-cellulose are not soluble to any appreciable extent, at ordinary atmospheric temperatures, in an excess of either ethyl ether or ethyl alcohol, when either is employed alone as a solvent? The point emphasized is, why should the single material, soluble nitro-cellulose, prove more soluble in a mixture of two solvents than in either solvent separately?

If one-tenth of a gram of soluble nitro-cellulose be

placed in a test-tube and covered with, say, 25 c.c. of ethyl alcohol, and the test-tube be corked and then violently agitated, it will be found that solution will not ensue, but that the soluble nitro-cellulose will (if pulped) gradually settle to the bottom after the tube is brought to rest, or else remain suspended in an undissolved state in the liquid. Similarly, the same quantity of nitro-cellulose will remain undissolved in, say, twice the same quantity of ether under similar treatment. If, however, the contents of the two tubes be combined, the soluble nitro-cellulose will promptly go into solution in the mixture of the two solvents.

Solubility in ether and solubility in alcohol must be touched upon before proceeding to the question of solubility in the compound solvent. It is known that certain nitro-celluloses of low nitration are soluble in ethyl alcohol. To this Vieille and Mendeléef attest, and the latter recommends that this fact be taken advantage of to remove traces of nitro-celluloses of low nitration from those of higher nitration, the higher soluble nitro-celluloses not being soluble in alcohol, at least not at ordinary temperatures.

If it happened that the soluble nitro-cellulose dissolved with the same ease in warm alcohol that it does in cold ether, the action of the compound solvent could be accounted for on simple physical grounds. A mixture of the two solvents might so balance differences of temperature as to effect solution at some temperature that represented a mean proportional to the percentage of each solvent in the mixture. The attempt was made, therefore, to dissolve pyrocellulose in alcohol (95-per cent.) heated to near its boiling point, but proved unsuccessful.   On the contrary, the tendency was rather away from than toward solution.   This theory was, therefore, untenable.

Having alluded briefly to the effect upon soluble nitro-cellulose of the individual solvents, (1) ethyl alcohol, and (2) ethyl ether, the solubility in the compound ether-alcohol solvent may next be considered.

In their work, "Cellulose" (London: Longmans, Green & Co.), Cross and Bevan, referring to cellulose and its hydration, state (p. 11):

" According to modern views on the subject of solution generally, and the solution of colloids in particular, the lines drawn by the older investigators of these phenomena are of arbitrary value; gelatinization being expressed as a continuous series of hydrations between the extreme conditions of solid on the one side and aqueous solution on the other."

In their physical forms the solutions of nitro-celluloses in ether and ether-alcohol present striking analogies to the hydrated and gelatinized forms of cellulose itself.   If, as stated, the gelatinized or hydrated form may be regarded as a continuous series of hydrations of cellulose, then the colloids can be regarded as what may be termed a continuous series of etherizations or alcoholizations of nitro-cellulose.   In this manner we may establish an analogy in point of behavior between cellulose in the presence of water and nitro-cellulose in the presence of ether, alcohol, and ether-alcohol.

Referring again to Cross and Bevan, "Cellulose," we find (pp. 4 and 5):

"All vegetable structures in the air-dry condition retain a certain proportion of water, or hygroscopic moisture, as it is termed, which is readily driven off at 100° (C.), but reabsorbed on exposure to the atmosphere under ordinary atmospheric conditions."

"The phenomenon is definitely related to the presence of OH groups in the cellulose molecule, for in proportion as these are suppressed by combination (with negative radicles to form the cellulose esters) the products exhibit decreasing attractions for atmospheric moisture. It is to be noted that some of these synthetical derivatives are formed with only slight modifications of the external or visible structure of the cellulose, of which, therefore, the phenomenon in question is again shown to be independent."

In parallel to this we may state:

The series of the cellulose esters known as the nitrocelluloses exhibit at ordinary atmospheric temperatures, with ether and alcohol, effects similar to those of cellulose with water in what relates to, (1) hygrocopic moisture, and (2) gelatinization.

In relation to the effect of alkalies on concentrated solutions—and this is of primary importance in connection with our subject—Cross and Bevan state (p. 23):

"Cold solutions of the alkaline hydrates of a certain concentration exert a remarkable effect upon the celluloses. Solution of sodium hydrate, at strengths exceeding 10 per cent. Na_2O, when brought into contact with the cotton fibre, at the ordinary temperature, instantly changes its structural features, i.e., from a flattened riband, with a large central canal, produces a thick cylinder with the canal more or less obliterated. These effects in the mass, e.g., in cotton cloth, are seen in a considerable shrinkage of length and width, with corresponding thickening, the fabric becoming translucent at the same time.   The results are due to a definite reaction between the cellulose and the alkaline hydrates, in the molecular ratio $C_{12}H_{20}O_{10} : 2NaOH$, accompanied by combination with water (hydration). The compound of the cellulose and alkali which is formed is decomposed on washing with water, the alkali being recovered unchanged, the cellulose appearing in a modified form, viz., as the hydrate $C_{12}H_{20}O_{10}.H_2O$.   By treatment with alcohol, on the other hand, one half of the alkali is removed in solution, the reacting groups remaining associated in the ratio $C_{12}H_{20}O_{10} : NaOH$.   The reaction is known as that of mercerization, after the name of Mercer, by whom it was discovered and exhaustively investigated. Although, however, it aroused a good deal of attention at the time of its discovery, it remained for thirty years an isolated observation, i.e., practically undeveloped. Recently, however, the alkali cellulose has been made the starting point of two series of synthetical derivatives of cellulose, which must be briefly described."

"From the points established by Mercer in connection with this reaction, the following may be further noted:

"At ordinary temperatures a lye of 1.225–1.275 sp. gr. effects 'mercerization' in a few minutes; weaker liquors produce the result on longer exposure, the duration of exposure necessary being inversely

as the concentration.   Reduction of temperature produces, within certain limits, the same effect as increased concentration.   The addition of zinc oxide
(hydrate) to the alkaline lye also increases its activity.
Caustic-soda solution of 1.100 sp. gr., which has only
a feeble 'mercerizing' action, is rendered active by
the addition of the oxide in the molecular proportion
$Zn(OH)_2 : 4NaOH$."

Two points in the above merit special attention in
connection with our subject.   They are:

1.—The removal of one-half of the alkali on treatment with alcohol, the reacting groups remaining associated in the ratio $C_{12}H_{20}O_{10} : NaOH$.

2.—The acceleration, on exposure to a lye of
1.225–1.275 sp. gr., of the process of " mercerization "
by reduction of temperature.   Here is presented an
analogy to the increased solubility of nitro-cellulose in
ether and ether-alcohol upon application of cold.

In referring to the production of cellulose thio-
carbonates and to the quantitative regeneration of
cellulose from solution as thiocarbonate, Cross and
Bevan state (pp. 29–31):

" The occurrence of this reaction, under what may
be regarded as the normal conditions, proves the
presence in cellulose of OH groups of distinctly alco-
holic function.   The product is especially interesting
as the first instance of the synthesis of a soluble cellulose derivative—i.e., soluble in water—by a reaction
characteristic of the alcohols generally.   The actual
dissolution of the cellulose under this reaction we cannot attempt to explain, so long as our views of the

general phenomena of solution are only hypotheses. There is this feature, however, common to all processes hitherto described, for producing an aqueous solution of cellulose (i.e., a cellulose derivative), viz., that the solvent has a saline character. It appears, in fact, that cellulose yields only under the simultaneous strain of acid and basic groups, and therefore we may assume that the OH groups in cellulose are of similarly opposite function. In the case of the zinc-chloride solvents there cannot be any other determining cause, and the soluble products may be regarded as analogous to the double salts. The retention of the zinc oxide by the cellulose, when precipitated by water, is an additional evidence of the presence of acidic OH groups; and conversely, the much more rapid action of the zinc chloride in presence of hydrochloric acid indicates the basicity of the molecule, i.e., of certain of its OH groups. On the other hand, in both the cuprammonium and thiocarbonate processes there may be a disturbance of the oxygen equilibrium of the molecule; and although there is no evidence that the cellulose regenerated from these solutions respectively is oxidized in the one case or deoxidized in the other, it is quite possible that temporary migration of oxygen or hydrogen might be determined, and contribute to the hydration and ultimate solution of the cellulose. But, apart from hypotheses, we may lay stress on the fact that these processes have the common feature of attacking the cellulose in the two directions corresponding with those of electrolytic strain; and it is on many grounds probable that the connection will prove casual and not merely incidental." *

It is the feature of *double attack* upon the cellulose that suggests the cause of the increased solubility of the nitro-cellulose in the compound ether-alcohol solvent, as compared with its relative solubility in the ether and alcohol separately. In the case of the "mercerized" cellulose we observe that a removal of one-half the alkali is effected by the alcohol treatment. The reaction of the alcohol here relates to the basic OH groups, the alkali appearing to be retained as a base in the groups of acid reaction. A lower temperature facilitates the "mercerization" process; this may be interpreted into the statement that raising the temperature of the molcule beyond a certain point retards the process. So, in the case of the increased solubility of soluble nitro-cellulose in ethyl alcohol at low temperatures, the employment of artifical cold accelerates the process of solution. We may here assume that the material, from its dual character, is under an electrolytic strain, from which it is removed by application of cold (abstraction of heat); the alco-

---

* Referring to the character of the regenerated cellulose in comparison with the original material, Cross and Bevan state, *inter al.*:

"(1) Its *hygroscopic moisture*, or water of condition, is some 3 to 4 per cent. higher, viz., from 9 to 10.5 per cent.

"(2) *Empirical composition.* The mean results of analysis show $C = 43.3$ per cent., $H = 6.4$ per cent., which are expressed by the empirical formula $4C_6H_{10}O_5.H_2O$."

It will be observed that the regenerated material is an *amorphous* hydrocellulose.

hol then attacks and dissolves the basic OH groups; the structure of the cellulose is destroyed; the acid groups yield subsequently and enter into solution, to effect which there may occur, as suggested by Cross and Bevan for cellulose, a temporary transfer, within the molecule of nitro-cellulose, of hydrogen and oxygen; and the whole substance finally yields to alcoholization in a manner analogous to that by which cellulose itself yields to hydration.

Similarly, for the increased solubility of soluble nitro-cellulose in ethyl ether at low temperatures, the employment of artificial cold accelerates the process of solution. The ether dissolves the acid OH groups (in contradistinction to the action of the alcohol, which attacks the basic OH groups); the structure of the cellulose is destroyed; the basic groups yield subsequently, to effect which there occurs a transfer of hydrogen and oxygen within the molecule in a direction opposite to that in which it occurs in the previous case, and the whole substance finally yields to etherization in a manner similar to that by which cellulose itself yields to hydration.

As bearing upon the theory it may be remarked that the two solvents, ethyl alcohol and ethyl ether, differ by $H-O-H$, since ether, $(C_2H_5)_2O, + H_2O =$ alcohol, $2C_2H_6O$.

In the case of the mixed ether-alcohol solvent we subject the cellulose in the one operation to the double tendency to disintegration. The necessity for the application of cold (or the absorption of heat) to effect the necessary arrangement of the $H-O-H$ groups, as they may be styled, i.e., to strain them into basic and acid relations, is no longer required, for the double attack in two directions, corresponding to those of electrolytic strain, is provided for by the parallel double composition of the ether-alcohol solvent.

There is reason for supposing that the above-described reaction is not limited in its occurrence to forms of soluble nitro-cellulose alone, but that it obtains equally for the insoluble varieties. If the theory be correct, then insoluble nitro-cellulose should be soluble in ether. Macnab has shown that insoluble nitro-cellulose dissolves in ether-alcohol at a very low temperature.*

In the fall of 1899, the time that liquid air first became readily obtainable in quantity in New York, I decided to check Macnab's experiment by employing this material as a refrigerant; also (1) to experiment with a view of ascertaining whether insoluble nitro-cellulose of very high nitration in its unpulped fibrous form,—the form in which it might be supposed to oppose a maximum resistance to the disintegrating action of solvents,—would not actually go into solution in ethyl ether alone under influence of extreme cold; and (2) to determine how far nitro-cellulose is soluble in absolute ethyl alcohol. The ether employed in these experiments was Squibbs', C.P., for

---

* See experiments cited by Guttmann in his article " Manufacture of Explosives," published in the *Journal of the Society of Chemical Industry*, London, June 30, 1894 ; also p. 404 appendix to his recently published work, " Manufacture of Explosives," London: Macmillan.

anæsthesia; the insoluble nitro-cellulose was gun-cotton of high nitration (N = 13.4 +) and purity, in the unpulped state.

The solvent employed in the alcohol experiments was absolute ethyl alcohol; the nitro-celluloses were (1) soluble nitro-hydrocellulose of nitration, N 11.4%; (2) soluble nitro-hydrocellulose of N 12.6%; (3) pulped pyrocellulose, N 12.42%; and (4) unpulped gun-cotton of high nitration, N 13.4%.

Experiment I.—I placed about one-tenth gram of gun-cotton in a test-tube, poured over it 25 c.c. of 2 : 1 ether-alcohol, tightly closed the tube with a rubber stopper and immersed it in a vessel containing about 750 c.c. of liquid air. When the contents of the tube became sufficiently cooled, the gun-cotton went readily into solution, forming a clear mobile liquid of a honey-yellow color. I found that the gun-cotton remained in the colloid form after the removal of the tube from the liquid and the subsequent heating of its contents to the temperature of the atmosphere. On removing the tube from the liquid-air bath, uncorking and allowing the contents to evaporate, the residue formed a tough, homogeneous amber-colored film.

Experiment II.—Having succeeded readily in colloiding insoluble nitro-cellulose in ether-alcohol, I next decided to ascertain whether it were possible to colloid it in ether alone. I placed one-tenth gram of the gun-cotton in a test-tube, poured over it about 25 c.c. of ether, tightly closed the tube and immersed it in the same quantity of liquid air as before.

Upon sufficiently reducing the temperature, the

contents of the tube became solid and the ether froze into a snow-white mass. On removing the tube from the cold and allowing the ether to melt, I found that the gun-cotton had disintegrated and gone into solution, forming a mobile slightly clouded liquid with a yellowish tinge. The gun-cotton remained in solution after the withdrawal of the tube from the liquid air and the subsequent heating of its contents to the temperature of the atmosphere. On removing the tube from the liquid-air bath, uncorking and allowing its contents to evaporate, the residue formed a tough, homogeneous, slightly yellowish colloid.

Experiment III.—About one-tenth gram of each of the above-mentioned series of nitro-celluloses was each placed in a separate test-tube and each had poured over it about 25 c.c. of absolute ethyl alcohol. The tubes thus partly filled were closed tightly with rubber stoppers, immersed in liquid air (for about two-thirds of their lengths), and allowed to remain therein for five minutes.*

The contents of each tube froze in about half a minute and the rest of the time the liquid air was acting upon the frozen contents. On removing the tube containing the gun-cotton from the bath and allowing its contents to melt, the gun-cotton was, to

* The liquid air for these experiments was very kindly furnished me by Messrs. Vandivert and Gardenhire, of 32 Broadway, New York, pioneers in the development of liquid air in the United States. I am also indebted to Mr. M. Burger, president of the company, for his kindness; and especially to Mr. O. Ostergren of New York, one of the original experimenters and developers of the commercial manufacture of liquid air,

all appearances, unaltered. This showed that, whether or not the fibre of the cotton had been attacked, it was not affected to the same extent by the ethyl alcohol as it was by the ethyl ether, which, as previously shown, destroyed the fibre of the gun-cotton, causing it to go into solution.

The sample of pyrocellulose and the two small lots of nitro-hydrocellulose in the other tubes were found to have gone into solution in the ethyl alcohol, through the action of the cold, the former affording a jelly-like straw-colored colloid; the two latter, the usual brownish-yellow colloids.

We may now call attention in parallel to the following remarkable reactions;

1.—That nitro-celluloses dissolve in ethyl ether under the influence of intense cold.

2.—That nitro-celluloses, with the apparent exception of the highly nitrated insoluble variety (this will be further experimented with later, in the presence of extreme cold) dissolve in ethyl alcohol under the influence of intense cold.

3.—That the so-called soluble forms of nitro-cellulose of mean and low nitrations go into solution in a mixture of ethyl ether and ethyl alcohol at ordinary atmospheric temperatures.

In connection with the above may be mentioned:

(*a*) That the various forms of nitro-celluloses seem more readily soluble in ethyl ether than in ethyl alcohol.

(*b* That a mixture of two volumes of ethyl ether to one of ethyl alcohol seems to extract at ordinary atmospheric temperatures the greatest quantity of soluble constituents from a mixture of the two forms of nitro-cellulose (soluble and insoluble as formed by one dipping of cotton.)

It now remains to consider the theory of composition of cellulose and nitro-cellulose from the chemical standpoint. In this connection it is necessary, first of all, to emphasize the fact of the similarity in composition of the cellulose and the nitro-cellulose molecule. The latter is formed from the former by the substitution, for a certain number of replaceable hydrogen atoms, of the same number of equivalents of nitryl—NO_2. The effect of the introduction of nitryl into the substance of the cellulose is an apparent weakening of the stability of the latter, rendering it susceptible of decomposition in a number of additional ways, and making actual tendencies to decomposition, traces of which exist in the original material, but which are held in control by stronger counteracting tendencies derived from other sources.

For the sake of simplicity the formulæ presented in what follows will be those of cellulose. It is to be understood that whenever questions arise referring directly to nitro-cellulose, such as solubility in ether or ether-alcohol, the cellulose molecule as presented is to be considered as tacitly representing nitro-cellulose, without actual expression of the substitution of NO_2 in the replaceable hydrogen atoms.

Bearing the above in mind, the following additional facts may be taken advantage of in formulating a theory of the composition of the cellulose and the nitro-cellulose molecule:

1.—The two solvents of soluble nitro-cellulose, ethyl ether and ethyl alcohol, differ in composition by H–O–H. Like H_2O, they may be written $(C_2H_5)_2O$ and C_2H_6O or $C_2H_5.O.H$.

2.—Cellulose, $C_{12}H_{20}O_{10}$, is transformed by treatment with alkali in aqueous solution into $C_{12}H_{20}O_{10}.2NaOH$.

3. By subsequent treatment with water it is converted into cellulose hydrate, $C_{12}H_{20}.O_{10}.H_2O$.

4.—By treating $C_{12}H_{20}O_{10}.2NaOH$ with alcohol, C_2H_6O, the former is converted into the mercerized form, $C_{12}H_{20}O_{10}.NaOH$, with half the alkali removed.

To account for the occurrence of reactions (2) and (3), the composition of the cellulose molecule is regarded as doubled, i.e., raised from $C_6H_{10}O_5$ to $C_{12}H_{20}O_{10}$. (4) is of especial importance and interest, as it exhibits the action of alcohol upon non-nitrated cellulose, establishing a basis for the assumption that the action of the double ether-alcohol solvent upon nitro-cellulose is based upon the original composition of cellulose itself.

Assuming a duality of composition as indicated (1) by its basic and acid reactions; (2) by its greater solubility in the compound solvent; (3) by the H–O–H difference of the components of the original compound solvent; and (4) by the creation and absorption of the H–O–H groups in the formation of cellulose hydrates and alkaline compounds, we may proceed as follows:

If alcohol is capable of effecting the solution of a nitro-cellulose, it must effect the solution of both its components or resolve itself into two sub-components,

each reacting on one sub-component of the nitro-cellulose, in order that it may effect the solution of the
whole. Under the latter assumption, we may consider alcohol, C_2H_6O, as having the composition

which may be divided into

Similarly, we may regard ethyl ether, $(C_2H_5)_2O$, as
having the composition

capable of dividing into

If such a tendency as illustrated above exists, it will become a reality through the disintegration of equivalents which, in combination, correspond to a molecule of water, H_2O.* The removal of one-half of the alkali from cellulose in the mercerization process is effected by the action of the alcohol upon the basic groups therein; the molecule of cellulose should, therefore, be represented so as to permit a resolution of the original material into acid and basic sub-components through the disintegration of the water-groups. Under this assumption, we may write cellulose as

---

* It will be observed that the constituents of water, H–O–H, form the central linking group in each of the expressions

which would resolve into

$$
\begin{array}{ccc}
\text{H} & & \text{H} \\
| & & | \\
\text{H—C—O—H} & & \text{H—O—C—H} \\
| \quad \diagup\!\text{H} & & | \\
\text{C} \!\!<\!\! & & \text{O=C} \\
| \quad \diagdown\!\text{H} & & | \\
\text{C—O—H} & & \text{H—O—C} \\
\| & & \| \\
\text{C—O—H} & & \text{H—O—C} \\
| & & \text{H}\diagdown\;| \\
\text{C=O} & & \quad\;\;\diagup\text{C} \\
| & & \text{H} \\
\text{H—C—O—H} & & \text{H—O—C—H} \\
| & & | \\
\text{H} & & \text{H}
\end{array}
$$

Form I.

or

$$
\begin{array}{ccc}
\text{H} & & \text{H} \\
| & & | \\
\text{H—C—O—H} & & \text{H—O—C—H} \\
| \quad \diagup\!\text{H} & & | \\
\text{C} \!\!<\!\! & & \text{O=C} \\
| \quad \diagdown\!\text{H} & & | \\
\text{C—O—H} & & \text{H—O—C} \\
\| & & \| \\
\text{C—O—H} & & \text{H—O—C} \\
| \quad \diagup\!\text{H} & & | \\
\text{C} \!\!<\!\! & & \text{O=C} \\
| \quad \diagdown\!\text{H} & & | \\
\text{H—C—O—H} & & \text{H—O—C—H} \\
| & & | \\
\text{H} & & \text{H}
\end{array}
$$

Form II.

The molecule as above written contains double central carbon bonds, which fact permits it, *on its entering into combination,* to be written as

```
      H                 H
      |                 |
H—C—O—H  H—O—C—H
      |     O           |
      C    / \          C
      |   H   H         |
    —C—O—H  H—O—C—
      |                 |
    —C—O—H  H—O—C—
      |   H   H         |
      C    \ /          C
      |     O           |
H—C—O—H  H—O—C—H
      |                 |
      H                 H
```

Without radical modification, it may be expressed

```
      |                 |
H—C—O—H  H—O—C—H
      |     O           |
      C    / \          C
      |   H   H         |
H—C—O—H  H—O—C—H
      |                 |
H—C—O—H  H—O—C—H
      |   H   H         |
      C    \ /          C
      |     O           |
H—C—O—H  H—O—C—H
      |                 |
```

as corresponding to $C_{12}H_{20}O_{10}$.

Halving it, we will obtain

$$
\begin{array}{ccc}
\text{H} & & \text{H} \\
| & & | \\
-\text{C}-\text{O}-\text{H} & \text{H}-\text{O}-\text{C}- \\
| & \diagdown\text{O}\diagdown & | \\
\text{C} & & \text{C} \\
| & \text{H} \quad \text{H} & | \\
-\text{C}-\text{O}-\text{H} & \text{H}-\text{O}-\text{C}- \\
| & & | \\
\text{H} & & \text{H}
\end{array}
$$

corresponding to $C_6H_{10}O_5$.*

This latter form, which is the simplest expression for cellulose, represents, not the molecule, but the type unit of cellulose, as it enters into combination, through its four free single carbon bonds, either with other similar units, by polymerization, or with other substances by chemical combination.

---

* Written singly, in a similar form, but with closed bonds, the single molecule, $C_6H_{10}O_5$, may be expressed as

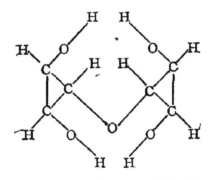

Compare also with Cross and Bevan, " Cellulose," p. 38, where, in reference to cellulose acetates, it is stated if the above formula (alluding to a formula cited) be established by further and exhaustive investigation, the cellulose unit must be $C_6H_6O.(OH)_4$.

The multiplicity of the cellulose derivatives and the generally recognized tendency towards polymerization already alluded to suggest the further amplification of the molecule by inter-combination of its units through connection of their carbon bonds into polymeric forms, the type of which may be expressed as follows :

Such a method of representation possesses a special interest, as it prepares the way for other considerations. The actual number of phases for the polymerized molecule thus expressed may vary from 2 to any desired number. In the above diagram a 5-phase form is presented for purposes of illustration. The simple molecule with its four free carbon bonds as presented in each of the five sectors combines with the simple molecule in each adjacent sector on either hand. The simplest polymerized form that, under our theory, can stand alone, is $C_{12}H_{20}O_{10}$, composed of two "sectors," the carbon bonds in each of which unite with those of the other.

Thus we have

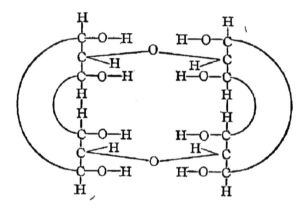

correcting the form previously written,

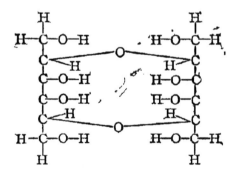

The 5-phase molecule, or its polymer, corresponds to pyrocellulose.

It is evident that under such an assumption the molecule may possess an infinity of phases. There is no limit to their number. On this assumption, and it seems to me on this assumption only, may we account for definite chemical composition of the cellular form in the plant structure. For we may regard the cell as built up from an aggregate of molecules of identical composition but of progressively-varying numerical phase. The cell may begin with molecules of low phase and end with molecules of high phase, or conversely. Molecules of progressively-varying phase-magnitude may be deposited in turn from protoplasmic matter in particular forms of different density, the successive evolutions providing for the infinity of cellular structures appreciable to the human eye, which, in their successive deposition, build up the fibrous substance of the cell.

It is to be remembered that the graphic representation of molecular arrangement upon a plane surface, —space of two dimensions,—cannot be regarded as more than a conventional device illustrating an arrangement that exists in nature in space of three dimensions. Nevertheless, the conventional ring-formed combination of elemental particles shown in the polyphase molecule strongly suggests the vortex-ring theory of the composition of matter (as applicable to the *molecule*). For whatever the *atom* may be, the molecule need not be limited in composition to the simplest collection of the *lowest possible number* of atoms capable of entering into combination, but may be built up from a very great number of the elemental particles taken together in their proper ratios.* Such

---

* On this hypothesis the atomic weight of cellulose would be represented by an average.

a molecule would increase in amplitude according to the number of elemental particles entering into its composition; and the thought therefore suggests itself, that *progressive variation in the amplitude of the molecular ring is a characteristic of organic life.* Or, conversely, we may state that we may seek for the beginnings of organic life,—at least of plant-life,—in the polymerization of the carbohydrates.

Briefly summing up, the conditions governing the formulation of cellulose may be stated as follows:

1.—The capability of the expression of the molecular formula as $n(C_6H_{10}O_6)$ or $C_{6n}H_{10n}O_{6n}$ justifies the assumption that the molecule may be represented as composed of n number of similar atomic aggregations of the form $C_6H_{10}O_6$, these aggregations conjointly forming the molecule.

2.—Under the assumption that Eder's nitrates represent limits of nitration in the sense defined by Vieille, n cannot possess a value less than 2; that is, $C_{12}H_{20}O_{10}$ represents the lowest expression for the molecule.

The fact that 2 : 1 ether-alcohol dissolves certain forms of nitro-cellulose at ordinary atmospheric temperatures with greater ease than any other compound solvent containing ether-alcohol in other than the 2 : 1 proportion, tends to show that all the OH groups in which nitro-substitution takes place are not similarly placed within the molecule.

4.—The fact that, at very low temperatures, either ether or alcohol singly will dissolve soluble nitro-cellulose, whereas at ordinary atmospheric temperatures a mixture of the two solvents is required to effect solution, implies that, under influence of cold (absence of heat), both ether and alcohol, on the one hand, nitro-cellulose on the other, may undergo a certain atomic rearrangement within the molecule.

5.—If symmetry of arrangement exists in the sub-components of the molecular section—$C_6H_{10}O_5$,—permitting the representation of atomic aggregations which, according to the influences to which they are exposed, may exhibit acid actions on the one hand, basic reactions on the other, it would be by groupings. of the carbon and hydrogen atoms, which are *even* in number, around the oxygen atoms, which are *odd* in number.

6.—There is good reason for the assumption (basis of theory of nitro-substitution) that the molecules of both cellulose and nitro-cellulose are of similar structure; that there is no general rearrangement of the atoms of the cellulose in the process of nitration, but that nitration is accomplished through the substitution of nitryl for replacable hydrogen in certain hydroxyl groups, the said groups retaining, after nitration, the position in the molecule that they held before nitration, as already stated. It is upon this assumption that we represent the molecule of cellulose as typical, both of cellulose and nitro-cellulose, and do not represent the substitution of the nitryl in the molcule, unless actually referring to some specific property of the nitro-cellulose distinguishing it from the original cellulose.

7.—Under the assumption (1) of the basic and acid, positive and negative, distribution of the atoms within the molecule, based upon the conception of the constitution of the molecule as a double salt, and (2) of the action of the compound ether-alcohol solvent upon nitro-cellulose at ordinary atmospheric temperatures, and of the action of both the ether and alcohol separately upon nitro-cellulose at low temperatures, we may regard (*a*) the ethyl ether, (*b*) the ethyl alcohol (which possesses the composition but not the atomic arrangement of an ether [methyl]), and (*c*) the nitro-cellulose, which possesses the characteristic properties of an ether, as all splitting up into dual sub-groups. The manner in which ethyl ether and ethyl alcohol could so split up symmetrically is easily shown; regarding nitro-cellulose as an ether, we may seek to split it into sub-groups within the molecule in a similar manner.

The three type forms may then be presented as follows:

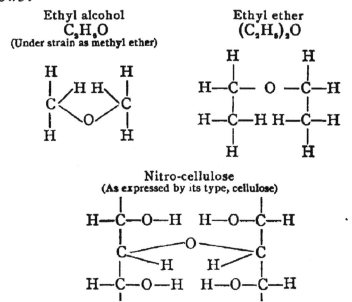

Ethyl alcohol
C_2H_6O
(Under strain as methyl ether)

Ethyl ether
$(C_2H_5)_2O$

Nitro-cellulose
(As expressed by its type, cellulose)

That all nitro-celluloses are soluble in the compound ether-alcohol solvent, notwithstanding the wide differences in temperatures at which solution is effected, leads me to the conclusion that all nitro-cellulose molecules are of similar constitution and organization. That they are of a dual composition is evinced by their more ready solubility in the compound solvent; again the fact that they are all soluble in the single solvent ethyl ether leads me to the conclusion that the two halves of the dual molecule are, with respect to each other, similar, or of similar inverted forms. Therefore, on page 60, Form I is the correct diagram of the separation of the factors, rather than Form II.

We have considered briefly in the preceding the composition of the molecule in relation to mercerization, polymerization, nitration, and colloidization. It remains to dwell somewhat more fully upon the reactions of nitration and hydration, and to show how they are reflected in the modified structure of the molecule.

The type cellulose has been written:

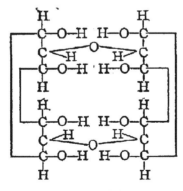

By changing the relative position of atoms of hydrogen, and without altering the constitution of the molecule, it may be written:

$$
\begin{array}{c}
\text{H--C--O--H} \quad \text{H--O--C--H} \\
\text{C} \quad \text{O} \quad \text{C} \\
\text{H} \quad \text{H} \\
\text{H--C--O--H} \quad \text{H--O--C--H} \\
\text{H--C--O--H} \quad \text{H--O--C--H} \\
\text{C} \quad \text{H} \quad \text{H} \quad \text{C} \\
\text{O} \\
\text{H--C--O--H} \quad \text{H--O--C--H}
\end{array}
$$

The polymerized molecule is composed of sections of the type:

$$
\begin{array}{c}
\text{H--C--O--H} \quad \text{H--O--C--H} \\
\text{C} \quad \text{H} \quad \text{O} \quad \text{H} \quad \text{C} \\
\text{H--C--O--H} \quad \text{H--O--C--H}
\end{array}
$$

From an examination of the unit of polymerization it

$$
\begin{array}{c}
\text{H--C--O--H} \quad \text{H--O--C--H} \\
\text{C} \quad \text{H} \quad \text{O} \quad \text{H} \quad \text{C} \\
\text{H--C--O--H} \quad \text{H--O--C--H}
\end{array}
$$

will be seen that the atoms of carbon are connected (1), by single bonds with each other; (2), with hydrogen bonds; (3), with hydroxyl bonds; and (4), with what may be termed " water bonds," of the form $\big\langle{}^{O}_{H}\big\rangle$.

Each carbon atom is connected with two other carbon atoms, one on either side. Every third carbon atom is connected with the di-valent " water " radicle (A). The remaining two of each set of three carbon atoms are each connected with one atom of hydrogen and one hydroxyl radicle (B). The symmetrical order of arrangement of the carbons is —BAB—BAB—BAB—.

The free carbon bonds of each unit represent *polymerization*.

The hydroxyl radicles represent *nitration*, in the mean and higher stages.

The " water " radicles represent *mercerization*, and nitration in the lower stage.

The open oxygen bond in the " water " radicle represents *colloidization* by combination of the half molecule of the nitro-cellulose with the half molecule of the solvent.

Nitration.—The process of nitration may here be taken up for more extended consideration. The fibrous cellulose reflects in its chemical behavior a characteristic of plant life, namely, the possibility of altering growth conditions through changes of temperature. The reactions into which it enters may be varied through the variation of the temperature at which the said reaction takes place. These changes in rate and character of reaction as due to temperature are especially characteristic of nitration, mercerization and colloidization; and doubtless, during the original growth processes of the plant, affect polymerization. The effect of temperature upon nitration is reflected in the resultant nitrated product in two ways: (1) in raising the degree of nitration in proportion to the increase in temperature (within certain limits); and (2) in increasing and modifying solubilities corresponding to given nitrations.

Until very recently, our actual knowledge of the nitration of cellulose may be said to have been confined to the following facts:

1.—That there was a lower limit of obtainable nitration, somewhere between that represented by the compounds $C_{12}H_{14}O_4(OH)_5(NO_2)$, for which N = 3.80, and $C_{12}H_{14}O_4(OH)_4(NO_2)_2$, for which N = 6.76.

2.—That there exists an upper limit of attainable nitration, somewhere near that of the hexanitrate of Eder, $C_{12}H_{14}O_4(NO_2)_6$, for which N = 14.14.

3.—That nitration is progressive between these limits; and that when determined at a given temperature, it advances gradually and progressively from the lower towards the higher limit, while under certain conditions it may be made, similarly, to decrease.

4.—That somewhere between the attainable limits of nitration a point is reached (and the point is not constant so far as relates to degree of nitration) where the nitrated product ceases to be soluble at a given mean atmospheric temperature in a mixture of ethyl ether and ethyl alcohol. This fact was utilized to separate the so-called " soluble" nitrates of celluloses of low nitration from the "insoluble" nitrates of high nitration.

Let us consider the formula for the double-type molecule in connection with the six nitrates formulated by Eder, and let us assume that there has been isolated from the substance of the cellulose for purposes of experimentation a homogeneous body

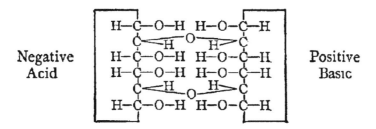

Negative Acid — Positive Basic

composed of molecules of the above 2-phase form. Then, if there are six nitrates, we could form them successively by substituting nitryl for the replaceable hydrogen in the "water" and "hydroxyl" radicles of the cellulose on *one side* of the molecule. Substituting thus in the above diagram we would have, for the highest nitrate

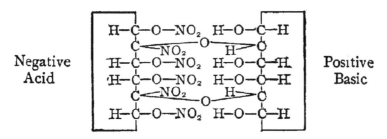

Negative Acid — Positive Basic

On account of the ready solubility of the lower nitrates in ethyl alcohol at ordinary temperatures the maximum efficiency of the 2 : 1 ether-alcohol, and the solubility of the highest nitrates in ethyl ether, we assume that the replaceable hydrogen atoms in the water radicles are replaced by nitryl first, and that subsequently the nitro-substitution continues through the displacement of the hydrogen in the hydroxyl radicles. If we regard alcohol as connected with the positive (basic) side of the molecule, and ether with the negative (acid) side, we may represent nitration, for the higher nitrates (say, the hexanitrate), as follows:

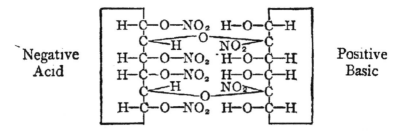

Under such conditions, we may formulate the nitrates of cellulose for the 2-phase molecule as follows:

TABLE V

Cellulose hexanitrate, $C_{12}H_{14}(NO_2)_6O_{10}$.
Cellulose pentanitrate, $C_{12}O_{15}(NO_2)_5O_{10}$.
Cellulose tetranitrate, $C_{12}O_{16}(NO_2)_4O_{10}$.
Cellulose trinitrate, $C_{21}H_{17}(NO_2)_3O_{10}$.
Cellulose dinitrate, $C_{12}H_{18}(NO_2)_2O_{10}$.
Cellulose mononitrate, $C_{12}H_{19}(NO_2)O_{10}$.

If we turn from the consideration of the theoretical 2-phase cellulose above represented to that of actual cellulose, we will find that the latter may be resolved into cellulose nitrates, not in *six*, but in a very great number of ways. Every molecule may be differently affected in the process of nitro-substitution. The character and composition of the resultant product may vary with strength of acid, its relative quantity in proportion to the cotton taken (this determines the rate of absorption of water formed during the reaction), the temperature at which the reaction takes place, and the duration of immersion in the acid bath. The cotton may be nitrated on the surface of the fibre or nitrated wholly throughout; it may represent a mixture of soluble and insoluble nitrates or it may possess a uniform degree of nitration; and it may exhibit variations (for the same chemical composition) in its solubilities in standard solvents; for the successive polyphase molecules are differently constituted and differently placed, and doubtless afford progressively-varying resistances to the effect of the acid bath.

It will be remembered that the theoretical limiting of nitration (14.14 per cent. nitrogen) was not obtained by Eder. Probably the ultimate substitution of nitryl for every atom of replaceable hydrogen is a limit that may not be attained in practice. Doubtless some of the molecules do represent complete replacement, while others are considerably removed from complete transformation. It will be shown hereafter that by colloidization the molecular amplitude of the nitro-cellulose is reduced to a mean, but such is not the case for the fibrous material.

Hydration.—When, in the attempt to nitrate cellulose, the strength of the acid mixture is reduced below a certain figure, a remarkable phenomenon may be observed—instead of a nitration there may be produced a hydration. We may, therefore, assume that from the same point of weakness in the molecule there may develop either a nitro-substitution (nitration), or else an atomic rearrangement accompanied by an absorption of water (hydration). It has already been stated that nitration starts, in accordance with our theory, in nitro-substitution in the water radicles, producing nitro-celluloses soluble in the alcohol (basic) solution. The hydration, then, should start in the rearrangement of the parts of the molecule adjacent to these water radicles. The quantity of water that is to be absorbed or, rather, taken up into the substance of the molecule, may, as shown by Cross and Bevan in their references to mercerization, approach the limit $C_{12}H_{20}O_{10}.2H_2O$; corresponding to $C_{12}H_{20}O_{10}.2NaOH$; while the definite hydrate, $C_{12}H_{20}O_{10}.H_2O$, containing half as much water, and corresponding to $C_{12}H_{20}O_{10}.NaOH$, is readily isolated. We have, therefore, as definite limits, the incorporation into the molecule of cellulose, $C_{12}H_{20}O_{10}$, of water in the two ratios, $2H_2O$ and H_2O.

Now the radicle $C\langle\,^O_{HH}\,\rangle C$ plus H_2O becomes

$$H-C-O-H \quad H-O-C-H\,;$$ and as the water radicle

occurs twice in the double molecule $C_{12}H_{20}O_{10}$, we have for the full transformation,

$$
\begin{array}{c}
H-C-O-H \quad H-O-C-H \\
C\!\!<^{O}_{H} \quad H\!\!>\!\!C \\
H-C-O-H \quad H-O-C-H \\
H-C-O-H \quad H-O-C-H \\
C\!\!<^{H}_{O} \quad H\!\!>\!\!C \\
H-C-O-H \quad H-O-C-H
\end{array}
\quad + H_2O =
$$

$$
\begin{array}{ll}
\text{H—C—O—H} & \text{H—O—C—H} \\
\text{H—C—O—H} & \text{H—O—C—H} \\
\text{H—C—O—H} & \text{H—O—C—H} \\
\text{H—C—O—H} & \text{H—O—C—H} \\
\text{C}\diagdown\text{H} \quad \text{H}\diagup\text{C} & \\
\qquad\text{O} & \\
\text{H—C—O—H} & \text{H—O—C—H}
\end{array}
\quad ;
$$

and

$$
\begin{array}{ll}
\text{H—C—O—H} & \text{H—O—C—H} \\
\text{C} \quad \text{O} \quad \text{C} & \\
\quad \text{H} \quad \text{H} & \\
\text{H—C—O—H} & \text{H—O—C—H} \\
\text{H—C—O—H} & \text{H—O—C—H} \\
\text{C}\diagdown\text{H} \quad \text{H}\diagup\text{C} & \\
\qquad\text{O} & \\
\text{H—C—O—H} & \text{H—O—C—H} \\
\\
\text{H—C—O—H} & \text{H—O—C—H} \\
\text{H—C—O—H} & \text{H—O—C—H} \\
\text{H—C—O—H} & \text{H—O—C—H} \\
\text{H—C—O—H} & \text{H—O—C—H} \\
\text{H—C—O—H} & \text{H—O—C—H} \\
\text{H—C—O—H} & \text{H—O—C—H}
\end{array}
\quad + 2\text{H}_2\text{O} =
$$

.

In considering these forms of modification of the molecular structure it should be remembered that the molecules of the original fibre are characterized by their variations in amplitude. And we know, actually, that hydration represents a breaking down of the cell-fibre. This breaking down is also illustrated in the two diagrams of the modified molecules just presented. In the former it will be observed that but one of the two water-bonds remains; in the latter, that both water radicles have disappeared and that the two halves of the molecule appear wholly separated.

The effect of hydration in breaking down the fibrous structure of the cotton and ultimately putting it into solution may therefore be explained by the following steps:

1.—The fibre exists as an aggregation of cells of varying amplitude. The solvent at first attacks those cells that are either the weakest or most exposed, and transforms in them some of the water radicles, $C{<}{\overset{O}{\underset{H\ H}{}}}{>}C$,

into the hydroxyl forms, $H{-}C{-}O{-}H$ $H{-}O{-}C{-}H$.

The result is a partial transformation into $C_{12}H_{20}O_{10}\cdot H_2O = (C_{12}H_{22}O_{11})$.

2.—As hydration proceeds, the attack takes place throughout all molecules irrespective of amplitude until in each molecule one-half of the water radicles are transformed into hydroxyl forms, and a material, yet fibrous, built up of modified cells of varying amplitude in each of which one-half of the water radicles are transformed into hydroxyl forms, results. This is the true hydrocellulose, $C_{12}H_{20}O_{10}.H_2O$, or, more properly, $C_{12}H_{22}O_{11}$.

3.—As hydration proceeds, transformation advances towards the total conversion of all the water radicles into hydroxyl radicles. This is accompanied by disintegration of the fibre and a tendency to enter into solution. The formula shows that with total transformation of the water radicles into hydroxyl forms the molecule splits up into two halves, between which there is no chemical union; therefore actual chemical combination of the two halves ceases, and there can be no chemical connection between them except such as may be represented by electrolytic strain.

4.—As solution becomes actually effected, the fourth and last, and perhaps the greatest, change in the series occurs. By their intimate contact and admixture the dissolved molecules, freed from their organic form of aggregation, are reduced to a common amplitude. They hereafter constitute amorphous cellulose, and may be represented as an aggregate of the form $nC_6H_{10}O_5$. It is probable, however, that the number of atomic particles in each molecule still remains exceedingly great, as progressive nitration still appears to occur for this material.

5.—The transformation of the whole substance of the cellulose into the form corresponding to $C_{12}H_{20}O_{10}.2H_2O$ represents the dividing line between the chemical and the physical aspects of the absorption of water into the substance of the molecule. Any greater absorption of water than that corresponding to $C_{12}H_{20}O_{10}.2H_2O$

pertains to simple solution; any less absorption, to chemical change, affecting the structure of the cellulose cell.

6.—The hydrocellulose obtained by the usual processes represents, simultaneously, a combination of all the above-described processes. Part of the cellulose remains wholly unattacked, and, if allowed to exist, renders the whole mass what the workmen style "woolly"; part is converted into $C_{12}H_{22}O_{11}$, a true hydrocellulose, which, inasmuch as its fibre still exists, combines to exercise the same effect upon the physical constitution of the mass as the unnitrated portion; part is precipitated as wholly hydrated cellulose of the form $C_{12}H_{20}O_{10}.2H_2O$, and part goes into solution.

7.—Once the fibrous structure is lost by solution, and the molecules reduced to a common amplitude, the organic constitution is gone and may not be recovered in any way. The cellulose thereafter remains as an amorphous body. This condition finds a parallel in the ultimate state of colloided nitro-cellulose, when the last traces of solvent are totally expelled therefrom, and there results a pulverulent amorphous mass.

APPENDIX I

RESEARCHES UPON THE NITRATION OF COTTON

By M. VIEILLE

VERY different formulæ have been suggested to represent the composition of the nitro-products derived from celluloses, and particularly the composition of products of maximum and minimum nitration. These products were, moreover, obtained by processes differing at the same time both as to temperature of reaction, concentration of acids, and the nature of the sulpho-nitric mixtures employed. Therefore the results were not susceptible of any general interpretation.

We have thought it well to take up this study again in a methodical manner, and to investigate the influence of different methods of nitration and of temperature upon resultant products.

I. FIRST METHOD OF NITRATION *

Conditions of dipping.—We first decided to determine the law in accordance with which the degree of

---

* In translating this paper I have converted the chemical formulæ employed therein into those of the system employed in the United States (O = 16).

nitration and physical qualities vary under well-defined conditions of dipping, namely, dipping in pure nitric acid of various degrees of concentration and at a temperature of 11° C.

The nitration was effected by immersing wadded cotton in from 100 to 150 times its weight of acid; all elevation of temperature was thus obviated and the strength of acidity of the bath could be regarded as constant during the whole of the dipping.

The operations were conducted in large-mouthed, stoppered flasks of about 500 c.c. capacity and cooled externally by a current of water. The flasks contained about 250 c.c. of nitric acid. Three grams of well-carded cotton were introduced into the upper part of the vessel which was then corked and shaken four or five times, whereby the cotton was equally distributed throughout the interior, so that each fibre might be considered as surrounded by 150 times its weight of acid.

Percentage of nitration.—The content of nitrogen in the nitrated product was determined by M. Schloessing's method for estimating nitrogen in nitrates. In order to apply this method to the determination of nitrogen in explosives, it had to undergo some modifications in detail, which show at the same time the degree of exactness realized in the conditions we have adopted. The following table presents a resumé of the reults of our experiments:

Density of HNO₃ T = 15° C.	Composition of the Acid	No. of c.c. of NO₂ evolved by 1 gm. of the nitrated product, meas 0° C.; 760 m.m	Character of Specimens
1.502 1.497	HNO₃ + 1.5 H₂O "	202.1 197.9	The nitrated product resembles cotton. It is completely soluble in acetic ether, very slightly soluble in pure ether or ether-alcohol
1.496 1.492 1.490	HNO₃ + 1.68 H₂O " HNO₃ + 1.85 H₂O	194.4 187.3 183.7	Soluble completely in acetic ether and in ether-alcohol. The fibre is not attacked
1.488 1.483	HNO₃ + 2.7 H₂O HNO₃ + 2.13 H₂O	165.7 164.6	The nitrated product has the same appearance as cotton. It becomes gelatinous through the action of acetic ether and ether-alcohol
1.476 1.472 1.469	HNO₃ + 2.27 H₂O " HNO₃ + 2.50 H₂O	{ 141.1 139.8 140.0 139.7	Cotton dissolves in the acid; produces a viscous liquid precipitable by water. The product thus obtained swells up through the action of acetic ether and becomes gelatinous without dissolving. Ether-alcohol produces no effect
1.463 1.460 1.455 1.450	HNO₃ + 2.50 H₂O HNO₃ + 2.76 H₂O " HNO₃ + 3.08 H₂O	128.6 122.7 115.9 108.9	The product is extremely friable, and is collected in the form of a paste. Neither acetic ether nor ether-alcohol produces any effect upon it
1.442 1.430	HNO₃ + 3.08 H₂O "	108.9	Residue becomes more and more friable, and is strongly blackened by the action of iodine solution. Nitration, insignificant

The number of cubic centimetres indicated in the third column corresponds, for each degree of concentration of the acid taken, to the maximum nitration.

Determination of the maximum nitration.—This maximum was determined in each case by the analysis of specimens exposed to times of dipping of increasing lengths. The limit is, moreover, very clearly indicated by employing a solution of iodine in iodide of potassium, which produces a black or greenish discoloration of nitro-products containing traces of non-attacked cotton. We may state that, beyond the point where the discoloration ceases to be produced, prolongation of dipping does not increase the degree of nitration. .

Thus a specimen dipped in acid of density 1.488 gave at the end of 24 hours of dipping 161 c.c., and was discolored by iodine. At the end of 70 hours it gave 165.7 c.c., without discoloration.

On the other hand, a specimen dipped in acid of density 1.490 ceased to be discolored by iodine after a dipping of 24 hours and gave 183.7 c.c. At the end of 128 hours the same specimen gave 183.8 c.c.

Nature of the reactions; speed of reactions.—The durations of dipping which determine maximum nitration vary considerably with the degree of concentration of the acid. The rapid action for the density of 1.500 (at the most from two to three hours) becomes gradually slower, and requires for the density of 1.483 as much as 120 hours. The corresponding nitro-products practically preserve the appearance of the original cotton, but for a density of about 1.470 the action is

completely modified, the cotton swells and dissolves
almost instantly, transforming the acid into a clear,
transparent collodion. If this syrupy mass is poured
into running water small white flocks are obtained,
opaque and brittle after drying, and which preserve
nothing of the primitive fibre of the cotton. In these
conditions the limit of nitration is rapidly reached.
Acid of density 1.469 gives after 5 minutes, 134.7 c.c.;
after 30 minutes, 140.5 c.c.; after 20 hours, 139.3 c.c.

When the density of the acid falls below 1.46, solution does not occur; the action becomes much slower
and the cotton appears unattacked, but it is shown
upon washing that the fibres become very friable. A
specimen was collected in the form of a paste. At
the same time the yields decrease very considerably
below the theoretical figure, which indicates that the
cotton has been partially attacked.

For densities below 1.450 it is no longer possible to
isolate, however long the dipping, a product that is
not blackened by iodine. The cotton is slowly transformed into products non-precipitable by water; e.g.,
at the end of 15 days there is obtained by treatment
·in water a very small residue which is intensely colored
black or blue by iodine, and which is of a very feeble
nitration.

Discontinuities in the progress of nitration.—The preceding table shows that, under the above-mentioned
conditions of dipping, the degree of nitration of the
cotton increases more or less gradually, in accordance
with the concentration of the nitric acid, from 108 c.c.
to about 128 c.c.; the degree of nitration then rises

to 140 c.c., corresponding to a very small variation in the strength of the acid, and it remains at this figure while the concentration of the acid increases to a very notable extent.   It again rises under similar conditions to 165 c.c., then to about 180 c.c., and then increases gradually to the limits of nitration of gun-cotton properly so-called.

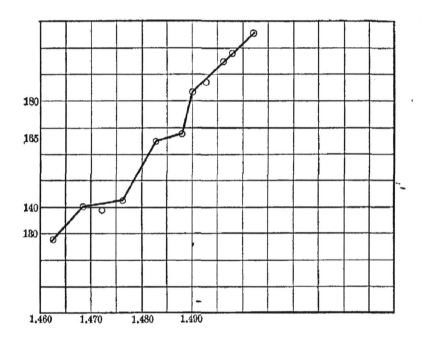

The above diagram, obtained by expressing the density of the acid by abscissæ and the corresponding percentage of nitration by ordinates, illustrates the character of the progress of the reaction.

The existence of these discontinuities is of great importance in relation to the establishment of the chemical formulæ of the nitro-derivatives of celluloses. It has therefore been deemed useful to reproduce these different degrees of nitration under entirely different conditions, employing sulpho-nitric mixtures.

II. SECOND METHOD OF NITRATION

We employed sulpho-nitric mixtures formed of ordinary sulphuric acid (density 1.832) and ordinary nitric acid (density 1.316). The conditions of dipping were identical with those which have already been described; 3 grams of wadded cotton in 250 c.c. of the mixture. The temperature varied from 19° C. to 21° C.

The following table presents a resumé of our experiments. The first column shows the proportion by volume of nitric acid to sulphuric acid taken:

Preparation of H_2SO_4 by volume for 1 vol. of HNO_3 $\Delta = 1.316$	No. of c.c. of NO_2 evolved from 1 gm. of the Nitrated Product at 0° C. and 760 m.m.	Character of Specimens
3.00	195.9	
2.50	190.1	
2.00	184.6 ⎫	Cotton not attacked. Soluble in
1.70	185.5 ⎬	acetic ether and in ether-alcohol
1.50	182.3 ⎭	
1.40	164.0 ⎫	The cotton is very slightly attacked (a little stringy). Soluble in acetic ether and generally becomes gelatinous by the action of ether-alcohol
1.30	166.7 ⎬	
1.20	166.0 ⎭	
1.10	141.2 ⎫	Rendered gelatinous by acetic ether. Is only swelled up by ether-alcohol
1.00	143.5 ⎭	
0.95	133.3 ⎫	Friable products
0.90	132.7 ⎭	

These results give rise to various observations.

The sharp advances in the degree of nitration indicated in the first method are equally to be observed under the second, and practically for the same contents of nitrogen, corresponding to a yield of 130 c.c., 140 c.c., 165 c.c., and 180 c.c. of nitrogen dioxide, approximately.

Thus the degree of nitration remains the same for proportions of sulphuric acid of 2, 1.70, and 1.50; and lowers abruptly by 18 c.c. for the proportion of 1.40. Nitration remains stationary for the proportions of 1.40, 1.30, and 1.20, and lowers again abruptly for the proportions 1.10 and 1.00.

In order to follow this phenomenon more closely we undertook dippings with proportions of acid intermediary between those for which the abrupt changes had been observed.

The specimens thus obtained gave the following results:

Preparation of H_2SO_4 by volume for 1 vol. of HNO_3, $\Delta = 1.316$.	No. of c.c. of NO_2 evolved from 1 gm, of Nitrated Product at o° C. and 760 m.m.	Character of Specimens
1.45	171.1	Cotton not attacked. Soluble in ether-alcohol
1.15	153.0	Cotton attacked slightly

The percentage of nitration is interpolated exactly between those indicated above. These trials confirm the preceding experiments, which show that the exactness of the mixtures under the conditions of our ex-

periments may be relied upon and that the discontinuities indicated do not arise from accidental conditions.
They show, moreover, that there are not, properly
speaking, sharp advances in nitration; and that there
exists a very restricted zone of acid mixtures with
which one may obtain intermediate nitration. But
there exists, nevertheless, a discontinuity in the progress of the reaction; and the following diagram,
obtained by expressing the percentages of sulphuric
acid in a mixture, as abscissæ, and the yield of nitrogen in c.c., as ordinates, allow us to keep track of the
progress of the reaction:

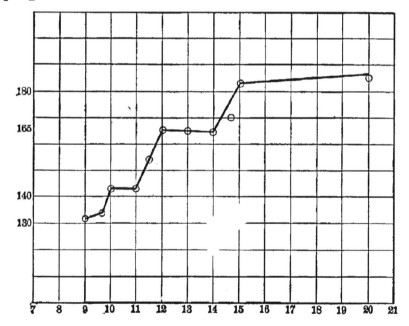

It appears rational to admit that definite products
correspond to the periods of constant nitration, and
that the mixture of the two products only occurs in
the intervals of transition. .

The properties of the cellulose nitrates obtained by the second process, in respect to solvents such as acetic ether and ether-alcohol, are, for a given degree of nitration, identical with those of the nitro-cellulose obtained by dippings in pure nitric acid. The properties of cellulose nitrates appear then connected with their chemical composition, and are independent of the method of preparation.

We have been able to establish this fact in a more rigorous manner by nitro-celluloses capable of conversion into collodions.

The zone of collodions, according to our experiments, is narrow. It comprises celluloses the nitrogen content of which is comprised between 180 c.c. and 190 c.c., approximately.

A little above this limit however, up to 195 c.c., and a little below, to 166 c.c. and often to 150 c.c., celluloses occur which are transformed into jellies by the action of ether-alcohol, and which filter by pressure through cloth. But it has been found that these substances do not produce fluid and limpid collodions useful in the arts; and on drying, collodions of low nitration have been found to yield an opaque and brittle film.

Now, all the nitro-celluloses capable of producing collodions, obtained from widely different sources, and which we have had occasion to examine, are capable, in accordance with their composition, of being arranged in the method that our experience has made clear to us. This is shown in the following table:

Collodion-cotton, Rousseau process....... 183.2 c.c.
   "   "   Billault-Billaudot...... 183.8 "
High-temperature cotton Rousseau, 1st lot 184.0 "
   "   "   "   "   2d " 189.0 "
Swedish gun-cotton for the manufacture of
   gelatin-dynamite....... .... 193.0 "
Swedish soluble cotton made at Vonges,
   in accordance with the directions in the
   aide-mémoire de la marine........... 185.4 "

III. HIGHER LIMIT OF DEGREE OF NITRATION

The higher limit of the degree of nitration does not appear in the preceding tables, which do not present results relating to a density of nitric acid higher than 1.502. Greater densities are difficult to obtain and, moreover, our first trials with an acid of 1.516 strength at a temperature of 15° C. resulted in a very marked attack upon the cotton. It is probable that dipping in acids of so great a concentration would only give good results at lower temperatures, but the upper limit of nitration of gun-cotton may be obtained indirectly by the use of sulpho-nitric mixtures. These mixtures, which were employed for the preparation of gun-cotton for military uses, produce products yielding from 208 c.c. to 212 c.c. of nitrogen dioxide per gram.

By proceeding with special care, we have been able at a temperature of 11° C. to exceed these limits and to obtain a product of 215 c.c. This limit remains exactly the same whatever the proportions of nitric or sulphuric acid employed, even when Nordhausen sulphuric acid is substituted for the monohydrate.

The influence of a great excess of sulphuric acid affects exclusively the rapidity of the process of nitration, which is thereby considerably diminished.

IV. CELLULOSE INCOMPLETELY NITRATED

The preceding results related to celluloses of maximum nitration, and the iodine reaction above indicated permits us to regard the latter as homogeneous bodies; but it is possible, by stopping the reaction arbitrarily, to obtain an idefinite number of celluloses of the same degree of nitration and of variable properties—mixtures of different nitro-celluloses and unattacked cotton.

Among these products we have made a special study of those which were furnished by the sulpho-nitric mixtures. On increasing the proportion of sulphuric acid in the mixture we may so slow down the reaction as to obtain for a given duration of dipping, say 15 minutes, any degree of mean nitration desired. The following table shows the composition of specimens submitted during variable times to the actions of different acid mixtures:

Composition of the Mixtures		Vol. of Nitrogen Dioxide evolved per gram	
HNO$_3$	H$_2$SO$_4$	After 15 min.	After 3 hours
1 volume	3 volumes	194.6	212.4
1 volume	3½ volumes	182 0	212.4
1 volume	4 volumes	150.8	200.7
1 volume	5 volumes	123.4	200 7
		126.8	200.7

All specimens which have been exposed to only fifteen minutes of dipping are blackened more or less strongly by iodine, which indicates the presence of variable quantities of non-attacked cotton; the second column of the table appears to show that the excess of sulphuric acid only affects the speed of the reaction, and that all products tend toward the same limit of nitration.

Moreover, we may verify the fact that from the very beginning of the reaction the products obtained are of maximum nitration, and that the results of rapid dipping in concentrated acids are simply mixtures of non-attacked cotton and products of the highest nitration.

Thus the sample which yields 126.8 c.c. treated in acetic ether loses 59.44 per cent. of its weight, and the residue presents all the characteristics of almost pure cotton; combustion, and coloration by iodine (black coloration very feeble in the presence of ferrous salts and hydrochloric acid). Only 60 per cent., then, of cotton is nitrated in this specimen; and if we compare the total volume of nitrogen dioxide, 126.8 c.c., with that of the cotton nitrated, we obtain 214.7 c.c.; which is the number that we would have found if the reaction were allowed to proceed to completion.

This method of dipping preserves the cotton fibre intact, which may be of importance in relation to the manufacture of nitro hunting powders, for it produces a natural and absolutely intimate mixture of gun-cotton and ordinary cotton. Moreover, the nitrated material obtained in this mixture does not differ at all from ordinary gun-cotton, and we may hope that it possesses a stability equal to that of the latter.

V. RESUMÉ AND CONCLUSIONS

Composition and formula of nitro-cellulose.—The first degree of *complete* nitration which the above-indicated reactions allow us to determine corresponds to a yield of 108 c.c. of nitrogen dioxide per gram, approximately. This reaction is produced with pure nitric acid and three equivalents of water. It is slow, and only gives a small yield, on account of the cotton being attacked under the hydrating influence of the acid, which is then the principal phenomenon.

As the concentration of the acids is increased, the per cent. of nitration appears to advance progressively to 128 c.c.; at least this is what the nitrogen content of specimens 12 and 13 of the first series (page 83) would appear to show.

It would be well, however, to maintain a certain reserve upon this point, because since these products are insoluble in the solvents, the iodine reaction remains as the only index of complete nitration; and it is to be feared that certain traces of incompletely nitrated products lower the percentage of mean nitration.

From 128 c.c. the percentage of nitration rises by marked increases to 140 c.c., then to 165 c.c., and finally to 180 c.c. Then, as the concentration of acid increases, the percentage of nitration rises progressively, by insensible degrees, to the limit corresponding to military gun-cotton, which yields 215 c.c.

In this last period, although there is no brisk change in the percentage of nitration, we may note the very clear transition point at 190 c.c. and 195 c.c., corresponding to the limit of the zone of the collodions.

In order to account completely for the different changes by the production of nitro-products corresponding to definite formulæ, it is necessary to quadruple the equivalent of cellulose. The nitro-celluloses which this formula leads to correspond to the theoretical yields of nitrogen dioxide per gram of material indicated in the following table, and with which we compare the percentages of limiting nitration observed, corresponding to the discontinuities of which we have spoken already, or else to a change in physical properties:

		Theory	Experiment
$C_{24}H_{29}O_{20}(NO_2)_{11}$..Cellulose endecanitrate.	} Gun-cotton,... {	214 c.c.	215 c.c.
$C_{24}H_{30}O_{20}(NO_2)_{10}$. Cellulose decanitrate.		203 "	215 "
$C_{24}H_{31}O_{20}(NO_2)_9$...Cellulose enneanitrate,	} Collodions. ... {	190 "	192 "
$C_{24}H_{32}O_{20}(NO_2)_8$. .Cellulose octonitrate...		178 "	182 "
$C_{24}H_{33}O_{20}(NO_2)_7$...Cellulose heptanitrate..	}	162 "	164 "
$C_{24}H_{34}O_{20}(NO_2)_6$... Cellulose hexanitrate..	} Friable cottons {	146 "	143 "
$C_{24}H_{35}O_{20}(NO_2)_5$ Cellulose pentanitrate..	}	128 "	132 "
$C_{24}H_{36}O_{20}(NO_2)_4$ Cellulose tetranitrate..............		108 "	109 "

It will be seen that these formulæ take suitable account of the production of limits of nitration and of all particulars presented by the reaction.

The approximate results obtained, however, are always lower than the exact volumes of nitrogen by about $\frac{1}{100}$. The differences appear to be attributable to the presence of a very small quantity of products of lower nitration.

Properties of nitro-celluloses.—The explosive properties of nitro-celluloses are in direct relation to the percentages of nitration. As the nitration diminishes the vivacity of combustion in open air decreases, and the production of carbonaceous residue becomes more marked. We may thus classify at a glance nitrated celluloses in one of three groups—gun-cottons, collodions, or friable cottons. The measurements of pressures developed by these different products in a closed chamber show that the force similarly diminishes with the percentage of nitration. Thus a collodion-cotton yielding 184 c.c. produces pressures inferior by $\frac{1}{6}$ to the pressure furnished by Moulin-Blanc gun-cotton affording 211 c.c. The percentage of nitrogen constitutes a true measure of the explosive qualities of a product.

Finally, we may mention that the stability of nitrocelluloses decreases with the percentage of nitration, with respect to reagents such as hydrochloric acid and ferrous salts. For products of low nitration the reaction commences when cold; for those of mean nitration a few moments' heating is required, but for celluloses yielding more than 200 c.c. of nitrogen dioxide per gram, the attack commences only after sustained ebullition. These products appear then to acquire the maximum of stability along with the maximum of power.

PARIS, September, 1883.

APPENDIX II

PYROCOLLODION SMOKELESS POWDER

By Professor D. Mendeléef

(Translated from the Russian by Lieutenant John B. Bernadou
U. S. Navy)

THE very favorable results obtained with pyro-collodion, and its adaptability to arms of all calibres, depend upon its composition and properties, which, for purposes of illustration, may be compared with those of other materials employed as smokeless powders.

As to its chemical composition, pyrocollodion may be designated *homogeneous*,* and herein consists one of its most important qualities. All previous and present forms of powder did not have or do not have this property to the degree here implied. From their very method of preparation, black and brown powders

---

* Homogeneity, in its full chemical significance, is not claimed, inasmuch as the composition of cellulose itself remains a matter of doubt. The quality is urged from the technical standpoint, in relation to the properties of other smokeless powders. It is possible that a solvent may be found capable of separating pyrocollodion fractionally; but pyrocollodion insoluble in ether or alcohol, but soluble in a mixture of these substances, is far more homogeneous than other forms of nitro-cellulose or any of the nitro-glycerin powders, inasmuch as the latter are readily capable of fractional subdivision.

are coarse mechanical mixtures, for which any consideration of homogeneity is out of the question. The same is true for those smokeless powders containing ammonium nitrate, picrates, etc. Nitro-glycerin powders may be regarded as gelatinous solutions of nitro-cellulose in nitro-glycerin, which, from their composition, are, chemically, non-homogeneous; moreover, various solvents (alcohol, ether, acetone, etc.) dissolve certain constituents out of them, leaving others.

The same may be said of present-day types of nitrocellulose powders; alcohol dissolves out of them the nitro-celluloses of lower nitration; a mixture of ether and alcohol, the collodions, leaving the excess of highly nitrated cellulose undissolved. Pyrocollodion,* however, surrenders no part of its substance to alcohol, while it is wholly soluble in a mixture of ether and alcohol. This chemical homogeneity of pyrocollodion, taken in the sense in which it is stated to be employed, plays an important rôle in its combustion; for there are many reasons for believing that in the case of the combustion of those physically but not chemically homogeneous substances, such as the nitro-glycerin powders (ballistite, cordite, etc.), the nitro-glycerin portion is decomposed first, and the nitro-cellulose portion burns subsequently, in a different layer of the powder.† It is to be added that the

---

* Under the assumption that the remainder of the solvent is wholly expelled from the powder.

† The experiments of Messrs. I. M. and P. M. Tcheltsov at the Scientific and Technical Laboratory show that for a given density

homogeneity of pyrocollodion possesses a direct bearing upon the uniformity of ballistic results developed by its use.

Besides chemical homogeneity, pyrocellulose and the powders prepared therefrom possess a second distinguishing quality, viz., that for a given weight of their substance they develop a *maximum volume of evolved gases*, the latter being measured at a given temperature and pressure. This new conception involves certain intricacies and complexities, and may be discussed to some degree of fulness, in what relates to nature and volume of gases evolved upon the decomposition of powder.

According to the law of Avogadro-Gérard, * the chemical equivalents or quantities of matter expressed by simultaneous chemical formulæ (e.g., $H_2O = 18$, water; $CO = 28$, carbonic oxide; $CO_2 = 44$, carbonic acid; $N_2 = 28$, nitrogen) occupy at a given temperture and pressure a volume equal to that occupied by two parts by weight of hydrogen, $H_2 = 2$ (its molecular equivalent). Consequently, if we possess the full chemical equation of combustion of a substance or

---

of loading, the composition of the gases evolved by nitro-glycerin powders varies according to the surface area of the grains (i.e., the thickness of strips or cords), a phenomenon not to be observed in the combustion of pyrocollodion powder. There is only one explanation for this, viz., that the nitro-glycerin, which possesses the higher rate of combustion (Berthelot), is decomposed sooner than the nitro-cellulose dissolved in it. This is the reason why the nitro-glycerin powders destroy the inner surfaces of gun-chambers with such rapidity.

* The development of this law is given in "Principles of Chemistry," by D. Mendeléef, 6th ed., 1895, chap. 7.

mixture of substances, of which the products are gases or vapor, it is easy to calculate the volume occupied by these products at a given temperature and pressure. For example: the combustion of black powder may be expressed typically by the equation:

$$2KNO_3 + S + 3C = K_2S + 3CO_2 + N_2.$$

Mol. wt, $2 \times 101 + 32 + 3 \times 12 = 110 + 3 \times 44 + 28 = 270.$
Volume in form of gases, $3 \times 2 + 2 = 8.$

That is, for 270 parts by weight of powder ingredients 8 volumes of gas* are formed, or 29.6 volumes per

---

* If the weights of the equivalents be expressed in grams we may ascertain the volume of gas evolved in litres, when the pressure P (in millimeters of the mercurial column) and the temperature t (in degrees Celsius) are known Thus as two equivalent weights of hydrogen and the equivalent of each gas occupy at a temperature $t = 0$ and a pressure $P = 760$ mm. a volume of $22\frac{1}{4}$ litres, then for t and P this volume becomes

$$22\tfrac{1}{4} \ (1 + 0.00367 \ t) \ \frac{760}{P}.$$

Consequently *one* volume, expressed in grams, occupies, approximately,

$$\frac{11.1 + 0.4070 \ t}{p} \text{ litres,}$$

where p corresponds to the number of atmospheres, each of 760 mm. at 0° C.; i e , $p = \dfrac{P}{760}$. Thus, in our example, if $t = 2000°$ C. and $p = 2500$ atm., the 8 volumes of gas produced by the combustion of 270 grams of powder occupy an actual volume of

$$8. \ \frac{11.1 + 0.0407 \cdot 2000}{2500} = 0.296 \text{ litre.}$$

At 0° C. and a pressure of 1 atmosphere we attain a volume of 88.8 litres for 270 grams. In this manner it is easy to proceed to the value V_{1000} given in the text, the actual volume of evolved gases per kilogram of powder.

1000 parts by weight of explosive. Brown powder (cocoa) represents (in its greater progressiveness of combustion and in certain other respects) a partial transformation from black to smokeless powders, and is characterized by the partial carbonization of its charcoal (which contains much hydrogen and approximates to a composition C_8H_4O), and by the small quantity of sulphur entering into its composition. Its mode of combustion may be expressed approximately as follows:

$$6KNO_3 + 2C_8H_4O = 3K_2CO_3 + 7CO + 4H_2O + 3N_2.$$
$$6 \times 101 + 2 \times 80 = 3 \times 138 + 7 \times 28 + 4 \times 18 + 3 \times 28 = 766.$$
$$\text{Volume of gases,} \qquad 7 \times 2 + 4 \times 2 + 3 \times 2 = 28.$$
$$V_{1000} = 36.5.$$

Or as follows:

$$4KNO_3 + C_6H_4O + S = K_2SO_4 + K_2CO_3 + 4CO + 2H_2O + 2N_2,$$
$$\text{Mol. wt.} = 516, \qquad \text{Volume of gases} = 16,$$
$$V_{1000} = 31.$$

It is evident, then, that the gas volume corresponding to brown powder is nearly 34,—greater than that for black powder; whence originates the preference generally accorded to brown powder over black.

In a similar manner we have for the complete (typical) combustion of nitro-glycerin,

$$4C_3H_5N_3O_9 = 12CO_2 + 10H_2O + 6N_2 + O_2.$$
$$\text{Mol. wt., } 4 \times 227 = 12 \times 44 + 10 \times 18 + 6 \times 28 + 32 = 908$$
$$\text{Volume of gases} = 12 \times 2 + 10 \times 2 + 6 \times 2 + 2 = 58.$$
$$V_{1000} = 63.9.$$

If we present in the same manner the decomposition of a type of nitro-cellulose of high nitration, such as Abel's trinitro-cellulose, $C_6H_7(NO_2)_3O_6$, we obtain the following:

$$2C_6H_7N_3O_{11} = 3CO_2 + 9CO + 7H_2O + 3N_2.$$

Mol. wt., $2 \times 297 = 3 \times 44 + 9 \times 28 + 7 \times 18 + 3 \times 28 = 594.$

Volume of gases $= 3 \times 2 + 9 \times 2 + 7 \times 2 + 3 \times 2 = 44.$

$$V_{1000} = 74.1.$$

If the typical combustion of this nitro-cellulose be presented by the equation

$$2C_6H_7N_3O_{11} = 10CO_2 + 2CO + 7H_2 + 3N_2,$$

that is, if we assume that water is not formed, and that the oxygen combines wholly with the carbon, then the V_{1000} remains unchanged, as the volume of gas formed $(22 \times 2 = 44)$ remains as before. Therefore we need not stop to consider how the oxygen is distributed between the carbon and hydrogen in the products of combustion, as the value of V_{1000} does not vary.*

If, for nitro-cellulose of high nitration we substitute Eder's pentanitro-cellulose, $C_{12}H_{15}(NO_2)_5O_{10}$, which

---

* It is another matter if a portion of the oxygen continues in combination with the nitrogen, or if the oxygen proves insufficient to convert all the carbon and hydrogen into gases; that is, if hydrocarbons are formed; but this becomes a case of incomplete combustion. Such conditions have a certain bearing upon the combustion of smokeless powders, especially when the solvent is not completely expelled; but, on the one hand, the quantity of hydrocarbons formed is relatively small, and on the other, they are formed (as also compounds of carbon and nitrogen, as cyanogen), in relatively small quantities, for all powders, even when the latter contain an excess of oxygen. In considering type forms of combustion there is no need of investigating secondary conditions of this class, especially as by so doing we are diverted from the direct study of the general problem.

corresponds to a content of 12.75 per cent. nitrogen, and to the composition of ordinary nitro-cellulose employed for smokeless powders, we obtain a greater evolution of gas, for

$$2C_{12}H_{16}N_5O_{20} = CO_2 + 23CO + 15H_2O + 5N_2.$$

Mol. wt., $2 \times 549 = 44 + 23 \times 28 + 15 \times 18 + 5 \times 28 = 1098.$

Volume of gases $= 2 \quad + 23.2 \quad + 15.2 \quad +5.2 \quad = 88.$

$$V_{1000} = 80.1.$$

The increase in volume of gas hereby realized is due to the fact that the quantity of carbonic acid evolved is diminished, while that of carbonic oxide is increased, which causes an increase of total gas volume, since, for the equation

$$C + O_2 = CO_2, \; V_{1000} = 45.5;$$

and for the equation

$$C + O = CO, \; V_{1000} = 71.4.$$

If we descend to a lower nitration and consider Eder's tetranitro-cellulose, $C_{12}H_{16}(NO_2)_4O_{10}$, we have no longer the case of complete combustion; for 20 equivalents of oxygen are required to convert 12 of carbon and 16 of hydrogen into gaseous products and vapors, while there are but 18 of oxygen available, unless we assume the products of combustion as CO, H_2O, and H_2.* It is known, however, that in the case

---

*In the latter case (without formation of carbon) the decomposition would be:

$$C_{12}H_{16}N_4O_{18} = 12CO + 6H_2O + 2H_2 + 2N_2.$$

Mol. wt., $504 = 12 \times 28 + 6 \times 18 + 2 \times 2 + 2 \times 28 = 504.$

Volume of gases $= 12 \times 2 + 6 \times 2 + 2 \times 2 + 2 \times 2 = 44.$

$$V_{1000} = 87.5.$$

But typical combustion, according to such an equation, is practically impossible; carbon and hydrocarbons are formed, and the

of combustion of carbohydrates low in oxygen, the latter combines with the hydrogen, from its greater affinity for that substance, leaving a part of the carbon deposited in an uncombined state. Consequently, such conditions do not correspond to complete combustion.

The formation of CO_2 shows that there is a certain excess of oxygen in pentanitro-cellulose; whereas typical combustion, corresponding to maximum gas volume, requires all carbon to be converted into carbonic oxide. Such typical combustion is afforded by pyrocollodion, the composition of which corresponds to the formula $C_{20}H_{28}N_{12}O_{49}$, as is shown by the following equation:

$$5C_6H_{10}O_5 + 12HNO_3 = C_{30}H_{28}(NO_2)_{12}O_{26} + 12H_2O.$$

Cellulose   Nitric Acid   Pyrocellulose   Water

combustion that actually does occur is intermediate in character to that expressed by the above and by the two following equations:

$$2C_{12}H_{16}N_4O_{18} = \quad C_4 + 20CO + 16H_2O + 4N_2.$$
$$2C_{12}H_{16}N_4O_{18} = 22CO + 14H_2O + C_2H_4 + 4N_2.$$

For the first, $V_{1000} = 79.4$; for the second, 81.4; the mean of the two latter is 80.4; of all three, 82.4. This quantity is close to that afforded by pentanitro-cellulose and pyrocollodion. In this manner may be explained the phenomenon that upon the combustion of nitro-cellulose containing a little less than 12.5 per cent. nitrogen, or of pyrocollodion containing a certain quantity of unevaporated solvent (which is equivalent to a lowering of nitration), results are obtained that approximate to those produced by pyrocollodion powder, although velocities and pressures are somewhat lowered. The existence of this phenomenon depends upon the homogeneity of the powder; whence it follows that it is better to have a content of a little less than 12.5 per cent. nitrogen with a homogeneous powder than a content of above 12.5 per cent. with the powder non-homogeneous, and that the best results are developed by homogeneous pyrocollodion of nitration $N = 12.4$ per cent.

In typical combustion it corresponds to the following equation:

$$C_{30}H_{38}N_{12}O_{49} = 30CO + 19H_2O + 6N_2.$$

Mol. wt., 1350 $= 30 \times 28 + 19 \times 18 + 6 \times 28 = 1350.$

Volume of gases $= 30 \times 2 + 19 \times 2 + 6 \times 2 = 110.$

$$V_{1000} = 81.5.$$

Before proceeding further, we desire to call attention to the fact that, whereas for brown powder we realize a volume of 34 approximately, we have here a volume of 81.5, whence, judging from volumes of evolved gases, pyrocollodion should prove $2\frac{1}{2}$ times more powerful than brown powder. Actual experiments show that the powders stand in about this relation to one another. In units of energy per unit for weight of explosive we have

	Pyrocollodion powder	Brown powder	Ratio
47 m.m. R. F. about	220	81.5	2.7 : 1
9-in. gun, "	223	90.7	2.5 : 1
12-in. gun, "	210	93	2.3 : 1

From this it is evident that our computed value of V_{1000} is in complete accordance with actual experimental results.

In this manner we may consider it as proven that, for a *given temperature and pressure, pyrocollodion develops a greater volume of gases* (and vapor) than is developed by black or brown powder (for which $V_{1000} = 30$), and even greater than is afforded by *powders prepared from the more highly nitrated forms of nitro-cellulose, and by the nitro-glycerin powders.**

---

* The rapid, simple and novel method of comparing the force of explosives herein employed was first suggested and used by me

In order to establish the full significance of the above deduction, it remains to show (1) that from the standpoint of practical applicability we can foresee no other material capable of developing as great a value for V_{1000} as pyrocollodion; (2) that the physico-chemical and ballistic qualities necessary in a smokeless powder are. developed by pyrocollodion, not in a less, but in an equal or greater degree than by other materials employed as smokeless powders; (3) that the estimate of ballistic efficiency of a smokeless explosive, through consideration of its volume of evolved gas, without regard to conditions of temperature, leads us

---

in 1892. It was developed through comparison of the composition of smokeless powders and of their products of combustion and of the results of experimental firings made at the laboratory. Although I see clearly that not only the volumes of products of combustion, but also their temperatures, must be taken into account in a complete analysis of phenomena attending the decomposition of smokeless powders, nevertheless I purposely give preference in these investigations to phenomena relating to volumes of gases evolved, not only on account of the simplicity of the latter and their direct accordance with ballistic results, but for the reason that with present methods for estimating temperatures developed by explosives (and these methods are unreliable) it becomes necessary to make numerous arbitrary assumptions (especially in relation to specific heats of gases and vapors at high temperatures), while for volume calculations we have definiteness of composition as a starting point; and if there be any assumption to be made, it relates to the distribution of the oxygen between the carbon and hydrogen, which, from the chemical standpoint, is not so material—and so far as it relates to volume it is of little significance. In all cases, however, I present but the elementary comparisons of performances of powders, as the fuller treatment of the subject does not constitute the object of my investigation.

into no error, although it would at first appear that temperature would have a direct effect upon the practical qualities of a powder.

Since smokeless powder was discovered, so many schemes were set afloat for meeting general demands, that up to the present time there remain as open questions which form of smokeless powder is the superior, and whether new and still more efficient forms may not be looked for in the future. In order to reply to these inquiries, it will be necessary first to glance over the compositions of materials capable of conversion into smokeless powders under the following assumptions: (1) That they leave no solid residue after combustion, and that their gases exercise no injurious effect upon the metal of guns; (2) that they undergo no change upon keeping for long periods of time, and contain no volatile ingredients; and (3) that they may be readily prepared in quantities sufficiently abundant for practical needs.

There are but few elements capable of producing gases that do not act upon metals, and, generally speaking, it is useless to try to find others besides hydrogen and nitrogen, and their compounds with oxygen and carbon, that do not act upon gun-chambers at the temperatures of combustion of powder. Therefore, in general terms, the composition of those mixtures or compounds suitable for conversion into powder may be expressed as

$$C_nH_{2m}N_2O_n.$$

The energy imparted to the projectile is derived from

the conversion of the mass of the powder into gases,[*]
the transformation being accompanied with the production of great heat.   These fundamental conditions
serve to limit the number of materials that are capable
of conversion into smokeless powder, the limitations
arising not only from the above-named practical requirements, but also from the chemical impossibility of
existence of many bodies which, if obtainable, would
decompose in the manner requisite for efficient ballistic action.   Thus, e.g., there does not exist, nor can
we look forward to the existence of, such a polymer
(in the solid or liquid form) of hydrogen as H_n, which
would decompose into hydrogen, H_2, with a corresponding production of heat.[†]

If we may not look for explosives among the simplest chemical combinations of the elements, we may
perhaps find them among those compounds of nitrogen and hydrogen which stand in the same relation to
ammonia, NH_3, as the hydrocarbons do to methane,

---

[*] And is not derived from an external source of energy, such as
the tension of a spring or the physical compression of gases, as
in the Giffard gun.

[†] If such a substance existed, then its decomposition, according
to the equation $H_{2n} = nH_2$, would afford a weight $2n$ for a volume
$2n$; that is, V_{1000} would be equal to 1000, the greatest possible
value. For nitrogen under similar conditions we would have
$V_{1000} = 71.4$, or less than for pyrocollodion. But the existence
of such a polymer is highly improbable. If argon (vid. Mendeléef, "Principles of Chemistry," 6th ed., 1895, p. 749) were the polymer of nitrogen, N_3, its conversion into nitrogen could only be
accomplished through the absorption of heat; i.e., it would find no
place in the category of " explosive " bodies (to which ozone possesses a relation).

CH_4. We should thus have, corresponding to ammonia, the series N_nH_{n+2} (e.g., diamide N_2H_4; triamide N_3H_5; etc.) and the series N_nH_n, N_nH_{n-2}, etc. As the representative of the latter we have, for $n = 3$, the nitro-hydric acid of Curtius, N_3H, which actually is a very explosive body, and which forms salts, e.g., with ammonium $N_3(NH_4) = N_4H_4$, which is also explosive, decomposing into the gases nitrogen and hydrogen with the evolution of heat, although ammonia itself is not susceptible of explosive decomposition, but absorbs heat in the reaction. If such compounds could be easily prepared, and if they possessed the qualities necessary to an efficient smokeless powder, such as non-volatility, good keeping quality, progressiveness in combustion, etc., they would prove especially suitable for conversion into smokeless powders, as the corresponding values of V_{1000} would be greater than for other powders. Thus we should have for nitro-hydric acid,

$$2N_3H = H_2 + 3N_2.$$

Mol, wt. $\quad 2 \times 43 = \quad 2 + 3 \times 28 = 86.$

Volume of gases, $\quad 2 + 3 \times \quad 2 = 8.$

$$V_{1000} = 93.0.$$

For N_nH_n the volume would be still greater, as $V_{1000} = 133.3$. But even if such products could be conveniently prepared from readily procurable materials it would be useless to consider them as available for conversion into smokeless powders, for the reason that they do not decompose through gradual or progressive combustion, which is indispensable in a smokeless powder, but detonate or decompose with extreme suddenness; hence, while they might prove suitable for filling mines or shells, they are unadapted for use in cannon. This property of progressive combustion or decomposition in successive strata is possessed only by those substances containing both combustible ingredients, and ingredients capable of effecting progressive combustion, such as carbon and hydrogen, which are consumed by the oxygen held in close proximity to them but which is not in direct combination with them.

The "combustion" of a powder is the union of the carbon and hydrogen of the mixture or compound with the oxygen that it contains, and with which it is in association, but not in direct combination. From what has been said already, it is evident that if the powder is to be smokeless and produce the maximum volume of gas, V_{1000}, it must evolve no other gases than carbonic oxide, CO, water vapor, H_2O, and nitrogen, N_2. If hydrogen be evolved, without the formation of the corresponding quantity (equal volume) of carbonic acid, free carbon may result, i.e., the powder will not be wholly smokeless on account of insufficiency of oxygen. If the combustion, as indicated by the equation, reveals carbonic acid or free oxygen (without the corresponding volume of hydrogen), an excess of oxygen is evident, and V_{1000} will not possess its maximum value.

We have, therefore, in the case of a composition or mixture $C_nH_{2m}N_qO_r$, the maximum volume V_{1000} for typical smokeless combustion, corresponding to two conditions: (1) When the content of oxygen, r, is just sufficient to convert the carbon into CO, and the hydrogen into H_2O, i.e., when $r = n + m$; (2) when the content of hydrogen is relatively great, as V_{1000} for H_2O equals 111.1, i.e., more than for nitrogen and for carbonic oxide, for which $V_{1000} = \frac{2000}{28}$ $= 71.4$. Moreover, all substances of the composition $C_nH_{2m}N_qO_{n+m}$ will develop volumes between 71.4 and 111.1, if the decomposition products be CO, N_2 and H_2O alone, as is required for rendering V_{1000} a maximum. Our problem becomes, therefore, the comparative examination of those bodies rich in hydrogen, for which V_{1000} may be greater than for pyrocellulose (81.5). We must ask: Are there not known substances, or mixtures of substances, rich in hydrogen suitable for smokeless powder? To answer this query, let us examine various definite compounds and mixtures.

Among the carbon compounds a large content of hydrogen is characteristic of methane (marsh gas), CH_4; also among the nitrogen compounds, or the ammonium derivatives.

Hydrocarbons of the limiting (saturated) series C_nH_{2n+2}* form nitro-compounds, and may, therefore, produce explosives. To methane itself, CH_4, there correspond mononitro-methane, $CH_3(NO_2)$; dinitro-methane, $CH_2(NO_2)_2$; trinitro-methane or nitroform, $CH(NO_2)_3$, and tetranitro-methane $C(NO_2)_4$. These

---

*See "The Principles of Chemistry," by D. Mendeléef, 1891, Longmans, Green & Co., London, Vol. I, p. 344. J. B. B.

substances are volatile as well as explosive, but all represent a deficiency or an excess of oxygen. As shown by V. Meyer and Professor Zalinski, the explosive properties of mononitro-methane are especially great when it is combined with potassium or sodium to form the metallic salts, CH_2KNO_2 and CH_2NaNO_2, which represent, so to speak, first homologues of the salts of nitric acid, since CH_2NaNO_2 — $NaNO_2$ equals the homologous difference CH_2. Experiment shows that this substance belongs to the category of detonating explosives, and is, therefore, unsuitable for use in guns (but suitable for mines).

If the decomposition proceeds without formation of free carbon (although there be but little oxygen), it should be as follows:

$$2CH_3NO_2 = 2CO + 2H_2O + H_2 + N_2.$$

If it be thus, then $V_{1000} = 98.3$, which is very great. But, as has been said, the substance is unfit for use in guns on account of its tendency to detonate. Besides, like other nitro-methanes, it is volatile, and for this reason is further unadapted.

The little known, but doubtlessly explosive, dinitro-methane contains an evident excess of oxygen, developing on combustion, $CO_2 + H_2O + \frac{1}{2}O_2 + N_2$, which corresponds to the relatively small volume $V_{1000} = 66$. It is evident that the excess of nitrogen and of oxygen combined with it in the NO_2, according to the known principle, does not increase but rather diminishes V_{1000}. The same is true for nitroform, $CH(NO_2)_3 =$

CHN_3O_6,* and for tetranitro-methane, the discovery of which is due to the skill of our eminent savant, L. N. Shishkov. Both of these substances contain too much oxygen to develop maximum gas volumes. A large value of V_{1000} would be characteristic of mixtures of products of nitration and of hydration (substituting the water radicle for hydrogen, $-H+OH$) derived from methane, as:

$$4CH_3NO_2 + CH_2N_2O_4 = 5CO + 7H_2O + 3N_2.†$$
Mol. wt., $4\times61 + 106 = 5\times28 + 7\times18 + 3\times28 = 350.$
Volume of gases, $\qquad 5\times2 + 7\times2 + 3\times2 = 30.$
$$V_{1000} = 85.$$
Or:

Nitro-methane   Methyl alcohol
$$4CH_3NO_2 + CH_4O = 5CO + 8H_2O + 2N_2.$$
Mol. wt., $4\times77 + 32 = 5\times28 + 8\times18 + 2\times28 = 340.$
Volume of gases $= 5\times2 + 8\times2 + 2\times2 = 30.$
$$V_{1000} = 88.2, \text{ etc.}$$

But such mixtures, although possible from the chemical standpoint, are unsuitable for use as powder, because their constituents are in part volatile; and this, apart from the consideration that liquid explosives are prone to detonation, which is more to be dreaded than formation of smoke, as detonation destroys the guns.

---

* As the typical decomposition of nitroform, we have—
$$4CHN_3O_6 = 4CO_2 + 7O_2 + 2H_2O + 6N_2.$$
Mol. wt., $4\times151 = 4\times44 + 7\times32 + 2\times18 + 6\times28 = 604.$
Volume of gases $4\times2 + 7\times2 + 2\times2 + 6\times2 = 38.$
† The mixture $7CH_4 + 3C(NO_2)_4$ presents such a composition, etc , but such mixtures are all as practically unsuitable for powder as mixtures of mono- and dinitro-methane.

Among the closely allied derivatives of methane as a hydrocarbon rich in hydrogen, the development of a large gas volume may be looked for from substances presenting the composition $CN_2H_6O_4$. Such a composition is possessed, for example, by the mixture of a molecule of formic aldehyde, CH_2O (or of one of its numerous polymers), with ammonium nitrate, NH_4NO_3, or the hydroxyl derivative of methylamine (i.e., CH_3NH_2 in the form $CH_2[OH]NH_2$) in combination with nitric acid, HNO_3. The typical decomposition of such a compound, if realized, would be expressed by the equation:

$$CN_2H_6O_4 = CO + 3H_2O + N_2.$$
$$\text{Mol. wt., } 110 = 28 + 3 \times 18 + 28 = 110.$$
$$\text{Volume of gases} = 2 + 3 \times 2 + 2 = 10.$$
$$V_{1000} = 9.09.$$

But such a compound either cannot be produced, or else is obtained only with great difficulty; or, as a mixture of ammonium nitrate with the polymers of formic aldehyde (e.g., glucose, $C_6H_{12}O_6 = 6CH_2O$), it develops undesirable qualities, such as hygroscopicity, a characteristic of all mixtures containing ammonium nitrate, and is therefore unsuited for use as smokeless powder.

Hence, after searching through all the possible combinations of the simplest derivatives of methane, we are unable to find among them (as also among substances containing no carbon) any suitable for employment in practice as smokeless powder, although we find compounds developing larger volumes of gas than pyrocollodion, and which may prove suitable for use in mines.

If we turn from substances containing one atom of carbon to those with two, three, etc., atoms to the molecule, we shall find, other conditions being the same, smaller values of V_{1000}, the volume decreasing the farther the limit is departed from, as is illustrated in the following table of possible, little volatile, compound ethers of nitric acid* and their hypothetical nitro-compounds, corresponding to the series of alcohols, $C_nH_{2n}(NO_2)_2$.

$$3C_2H_4(NO_3)_2 + 2C_2H_6O_2 \qquad V_{1000} = \tfrac{60}{680} \; 1000 = 86.2$$
$$C_3H_6(NO_3)_2 \qquad\qquad\quad " \;\; = \tfrac{14}{166} \; 1000 = 84.3$$
$$C_4H_8(NO_3)_2 + 4C_4H_7(NO_2)(NO_3)_2 \;\; " \;\; = \tfrac{89}{1074} \; 1000 = 83\,7$$
$$C_5H_{10}(NO_3)_2 + 4C_5H_8(NO_2)_2(NO_3)_2 \;\; " \;\; = \tfrac{110}{1330} \; 1000 = 82.7$$

etc., etc.

The possible, yet up to the present, hypothetical, nitric ethers of nitro-glucol, although capable of developing large values of V_{1000}, and adaptable on account of their non-volatility, possess no advantages over derivatives of the higher alcohols, such as glycerin and mannite, materials that are readily obtainable as they are widely disseminated throughout nature. We shall therefore fix our attention upon the latter, first, as they present in their analogues substances extremely rich in hydrogen, capable of producing large values of V_{1000}; and second, because they are easily re-

---

*Considered by themselves these ethers of diatomic limiting (saturated) alcohols $C_nH_{2n}(NO_3)_2$ consume into CO and H_2O only for $n = 3$. For greater values of n there is a deficiency in oxygen; for $n = 2$, an excess. We have chosen them as an example on account of their slight volatility, and because they approximate nitro-glycerin and nitro-mannite in composition.

acted upon by nitric acid, forming the explosive compound ethers, nitro-glycerin, $C_6H_6(NO_2)_3 = C_6H_5N_3O_9$, and nitro-mannite, $C_6H_8(NO_2)_6O_6 = C_6H_8N_6O_{18}$. Both of these nitro-derivatives are easily prepared. The former was first employed as an explosive by the renowned Russian chemist N. N. Zinin, at the time of the Crimean war, and subsequently by V. F. Petrushevski, in the sixties, before the discovery and very general employment of Nobel's dynamite and other nitro-glycerin preparations; the cause of their general use being the ease with which the base material—glycerin—was obtainable in nature, while the reaction with nitric acid (admixed with sulphuric) was easily effected, i.e., the manufacturing process was a simple one.

Nitro-mannite, isolated and investigated by N. N. Sokolov, professor at the Medico-Chirurgical Academy, is also easily prepared, but not in its lower degrees of nitration. This circumstance is important, for the reason that the readily manufactured nitro-glycerin and nitro-mannite are not themselves available for use in guns, although very well adapted for detonating effects. They correspond, moreover, to relatively small values of V_{1000}, as they contain an excess of oxygen:

$$C_3H_5(NO_3)_3 \text{ affords } V_{1000} = 63.9.$$
$$C_6H_8(NO_3)_6 \quad `` \quad V_{1000} = 61.9.$$

But as these substances contain an excess of oxygen, they may be admixed with others containing a deficiency thereof, and which they consume, evolving carbonic oxide and developing relatively large volumes, V_{1000}; while by admixture with such substances, low in oxygen, or not containing it; their detonating qualities may be caused to diminish, or made to vanish, as in dynamite, by combination with an inert base (tripoli, magnesia, etc.), whereby the tendency of nitro-glycerin to detonation through shock is diminished. In this manner, by admixture with a combustible substance, nitro-glycerin powders are formed. If we take cordite as an example, we find that on account of its excess of oxygen it produces a relatively small gas volume; we may, therefore, select a mixture of nitro-glycerin and collodion (assumed as $C_9H_8[NO_2]_2O_9$) such as ballistite and determine for it V_{1000} on the assumption that it shall develop only CO, H_2O and N_2.

$$2C_3H_5N_3O_9 + 7C_9H_8N_2O_9 = 48CO + 33H_2O + 10N_2.$$
$$\text{Mol. wt. } 2 \times 227 + 7 \times 252 = 48 \times 28 + 33 \times 18 + 10 \times 28 = 2218.$$
$$\text{Volume of gases} = 48 \times 2 + 33 \times 2 + 10 \times 2 = 182.$$
$$V_{1000} = 82.1.$$

Therefore, if nitro-glycerin powders contain only the quantity of nitro-glycerin necessary to produce H_2O and CO, then the volume of gases evolved by them is almost the same as that developed by pyrocollodion. It is evident, then, that neither nitro-glycerin nor its mixtures, when employed as smokeless powder, evolve volumes of gases greater than pyrocollodion, and that admixture with other substances, of whatever kind they may be, although homogeneous from the mechanical standpoint, are still far less homogeneous than any single substance, and that it is useless to seek for nitro-glycerin powders capable of exceeding pyrocollodion powders in point of magnitude of V_{1000}, apart from other considerations. This applies also to nitro-mannite, the source of preparation of which is far less common than glycerin, and to many of the hydrocarbons analogous thereto, as glucose, starch, cellulose, etc. If all of the six atoms of carbon in mannite are in the same combination as in the limiting (saturated) alcohols:

$$C_6H_{14}O_6 =$$
$$CH_2(OH)CH(OH)CH(OH)CH(OH)CH(OH)CH_2(OH),$$

then in glucose, $C_6H_{12}O_6$, one atom of carbon should be combined as in aldehyde,

$$C_6H_{12}O_6 =$$
$$COH\ CH(OH)CH(OH)CH(OH)CH(OH)CH_2(OH),$$

and, therefore, if mannite represents a hexanitrated product (compound ether as derived from an alcohol), glucose represents only a pentanitrate. Materials such as cellulose, starch, and the like, of composition $C_6H_{10}O_5$, may be regarded as the preceding alcohols—anhydrous, arranged as follows with reference to the di-alcoholic groups:

$$C_6H_{10}O_5 = COH\ CH(OH)\ CH(OH)\ CH(OH)\overbrace{}^{\text{CH CH}_2}_{O},$$

whereby it appears that there are only three complete alcohol groups remaining out of the six in mannite. Therefore, in the latter case, we should expect to find only trinitrated products, which is actually what occurs. If such a scheme throws light on the matter from one standpoint (as relates to the number of hydroxyl radicles giving rise to nitric ethers), it illuminates it obliquely from another, which is of considerable importance to us. In all aldehydes, beginning with the formic and acetic, a tendency to polymerization is to be noted, due, doubtless, to the property of aldehydes of entering into various combinations (with H_2, O, $NaHSO_3$, etc.); hence the composition $C_6H_{10}O_5$, containing an aldehyde grouping, should also possess this property, so far as relates thereto. We may, therefore, safely assume that the molecular composition of cellulose, judging from its properties, is polymerized, i.e., it is of the form $C_{6n}H_{10n}O_{5n}$, where n is probably very great. If we assume $n = 5$, the cellulose becomes of composition $C_{30}H_{50}O_{25}$, and, for the highest degree of nitration, $C_{30}H_{35}(NO_2)_{15}O_{25}$. But pyrocellulose has a composition $C_{30}H_{38}(NO_2)_{12}O_{25}$; therefore, the number of independent nitro-celluloses (nitric ethers) may be very large.

This is very important in the conception that the nitration of cellulose may be carried up to any desired degree, and for known concentrations a mixture of nitric and sulphuric acids neither dissolves nor reacts upon a product of nitration. Again, cellulose is the most widely disseminated in nature of all the hydrocarbons possessing the composition $C_6H_{10}O_5$, constituting the tissues of all plants and prepared from time immemorial in great masses as cotton, flax, paper, etc., while its products of nitration present an unalterable material suitable for conversion into smokeless

powder. This side of the matter needs no further
elucidation, but it must be remembered that before
the development of pyrocollodion, it was stated that
the higher the nitration of the cellulose the higher the
explosive produced, and that in manufacturing powder.
from highly explosive nitro-cellulose (of composition
about $C_{30}H_{36}[NO_2]_{14}O_{26}$), collodion (of composition about
$C_{30}H_{40}[NO_2]_{10}O_{26}$) was added, for the reason that higher
nitro-celluloses in the form of filaments or dust were
easily detonated (hence their employment for mines),
while the latter property was reduced or caused to disappear after gelatinization, of which collodion was
easily susceptible and for which purpose it was added.
The introduction of pyrocollodion changed existing
views upon the subject, showing that maximum force
for nitro-cellulose was not to be sought from the highest degrees of nitration (i.e., for maximum content of
nitrogen and oxygen), but that it obtained for that
mean degree of nitration present in pyrocollodion.
For the latter material $V_{1000} = 81.5$; while for nitro-
cellulose of maximum nitration, $C_6N_7(NO_2)_5O_6$, $V_{1000} =$
74.1. The above represents only one side of the theoretical investigation of materials suitable for smokeless powder; but other considerations are also in ac-
cord, as will be shown later; and we have, therefore,
gone considerably into detail, the more urgently since
it has been necessary to struggle with prejudice,
harmful to success in such a new field as that of
smokeless powders.

Among the possible materials proposed, apart from
mixtures of such different bodies as ammonium nitrate

and various organic substances (such mixtures were rejected in practice), must be considered the nitro-compounds corresponding to benzol and its derivatives, naphtalin, etc., as coal-tar constitutes an abundant source for their production in large quantities, and they are easily nitrated. From the class of the so-called "aromatic compounds" derived from benzol, C_6H_6, it is useless to expect smokeless explosives developing large volumes of V_{1000}, although many are high explosives, beginning with Melinite or picric acid, $C_6H_3(NO_2)_3OH$, which constitutes a powerful material, although far from the best, for torpedoes and explosive shells; and since some of the first smokeless powders were mixtures containing picric acid. The cause of the small gas volumes V_{1000} developed by the aromatic compounds is due to their composition, as they are all low in hydrogen. This view may be illustrated by a few examples.

To benzol there correspond bodies the general composition of which may be expressed by the formula $C_6H_{6-a}(NO_2)_a$. If a equals 1, 2 or 3 (these substances are known and easily obtained), the oxygen content is insufficient to consume the carbon into CO and the hydrogen into H_2O, although explosion occurs with the formation of carbon (smoke, soot) and of hydrocarbons.

Total smokelessness could be realized from mixtures of highly nitrated products, as:

$$4C_6H_2(NO_2)_4 + C_6H_4(NO_2)_2 = 30CO + 6H_2O + 9N_2.$$

Mol. wt., $4 \times 258 + 168 = 30 \times 28 + 6 \times 18 + 9 \times 28 = 1200$.

Volume of gases $= 30 \times 2 + 6 \times 2 + 9 \times 2 = 90$.

$$V_{1000} = 75.$$

If, instead of such non-existing highly nitrated benzols, pyroxylin be employed (as in the American smokeless powders of Munroe and other inventors), a gas volume approaching that developed by pyrocollodion is realized:

$$6C_6H_5NO_2 + 26C_6H_7N_3O_{11} = 192CO + 106H_2O + 42N_2.$$

Mol. wt., $6 \times 123 + 26 \times 297 = 192 \times 28 + 106 \times 18 + 42 \times 28 = 8460.$

Volume of gases $= 193 \times 2 + 106 \times 2 + 42 \times 2 = 680.$

$$V_{1000} = 80.4.$$

The matter assumes a different aspect if ammonium nitrate, NH_4NO_3, be employed for converting the carbon and hydrogen of nitro-benzol into CO and H_2O. This substance contains a large quantity of hydrogen for a relatively small content of oxygen (but for this result a large quantity of NH_4NO_3 must enter into the mixture), and greatly increases the volume of gas developed, as is evident from the following:

$$2C_6H_5NO_2 + 13NH_4NO_3 = 12CO + 31H_2O + 14N_2.$$

Mol. wt., $2 \times 123 + 13 \times 80 = 12 \times 28 + 31 \times 18 + 14 \times 28 = 1286.$

Volume of gases $= 12 \times 2 + 31 \times 2 + 14 \times 2 = 114.$

$$V_{1000} = 88.7.$$

But mixtures of this salt must always be avoided if a satisfactory smokeless powder is to be produced, as it is soluble in water, as well as hygroscopic, and produces with viscous, oily materials only coarse mechanical mixtures.

Similar results are to be obtained from other aromatic substances, and we may refer by way of example to mixtures of pyroxylin with picric acid, $C_6H_2(NO_2)_3OH$, and nitro-naphtalin, $C_{10}H_7(NO_2)$, such compounds having been recently experimented with (but abandoned in practice) as smokeless powders. Among other disadvantages, they develop smaller gas volumes, V_{1000}, than pyrocollodion, on account of their relatively small content of hydrogen.

After an examination in the above manner of the composition and properties of all possible materials capable of employment as smokeless powders, we arrive at the following deductions in relation to the volume of gases (measured at given temperature and pressure), V_{1000}, developed by their combustion:

1.—Only substances containing nitrogen, carbon, hydrogen and oxygen are capable of entire conversion, as required for smokeless powders, into gases that do not react upon gun-metals. Hence all other explosive substances (e.g., fulminate of mercury, chloride of nitrogen, etc.) containing haloids, metals, phosphorus, etc., are unsuitable for use in gunpowders.

2.—When the combustion of carbon results in the formation of carbonic acid gas, CO_2, a less volume of gas is formed than when carbonic oxide, CO, is the resultant product; and as the former requires more oxygen than the latter, the increase of oxygen or nitrogen (if, as is usually the case, the oxygen enters into combination with the aid of the elements of nitric acid) is injurious, instead of useful, although there exists full conversion into gases as is required for smokeless powder.

3.—The greater the quantity of hydrogen in the powder, other conditions being equal, the greater the gas volume, V_{1000}, corresponding to the combustion of the powder; and, therefore, substances derived from the limiting (saturated) series of hydrocarbons are more suitable than bodies of the "aromatic" series for smokeless powders.

4.—Not any of these explosive materials not containing carbon (as N_3H, NH_4NO_2), that evolve large volumes of gas V_{1000} and decompose upon ignition, are such as will not detonate, i.e., evolve their gases so rapidly that they crush the walls of guns; whence it is useless to consider them as materials adaptable for conversion into smokeless powders.

5.—Some of the materials containing but little carbon and much hydrogen may prove suitable for use as powders or powder mixtures, evolving large volumes of gas upon combustion; but, so far as known, they are either volatile, or liable to decompose spontaneously and detonate, or else they are prepared with difficulty from mixtures not widely disseminated, so that at present it is useless to look for materials for smokeless powder from among them.

6.—Nitro-glycerin itself develops but a small gas volume ($V_{1000} = 63.9$), as it contains an excess of oxygen. It may be employed in mixtures to form smokeless powder, and its mixtures with nitro-cellulose, such as Cordite and Ballistite, which are practically homogeneous from a physical standpoint, develop gas volumes, V_{1000} a little less than that evolved by pyrocollodion (although such mixtures erode guns, as already stated).

7.—Cellulose, $C_{6n}H_{10n}O_{5n}$, is a substance widely disseminated in nature and of general industrial employment; by its non-volatility, insolubility, durability, etc., and by the readiness with which it is nitrated (as it contains much hydrogen), it constitutes a superior base for smokeless powders.

8.—Among all the forms of nitro-cellulose capable of smokeless combustion, the maximum gas volume, V_{1000}, corresponds to $C_{30}H_{38}N_{12}O_{49}$ ($= 12.44$ per cent. nitrogen), which is pyrocollodion, for which $V_{1000} = 81.5$, and which is capable of complete gelatinization in a mixture of ether and alcohol, in which form it is completely free from any tendency to detonate. In the first place, it is the most suitable of all the nitro-celluloses; in the second, it is the most rational and readily obtainable form of smokeless powder, destined to supplant not only other smokeless powders, but also to replace, by reason of its greater homogeneity and its combination of qualities, other pyroxylin powders.

Pyroxylin powder is a mixture of nitro-celluloses, of higher nitration, such as $C_6H_7(NO_2)_3O_5$, and of lower, as $C_6H_8(NO_2)_2O_5$; pyrocollodion is a definite homogeneous single form of nitrocellulose. By changing the proportional relation of contents of the high, or insoluble, and low, or soluble, nitro-cellulose, it is evidently possible to make the pyroxylin approach the pyrocollodion powders; but (as has been shown in recent years, especially in cannon-powders) the limit of improvement of these forms always falls short of pyrocollodion. The latter is homogeneous and unchangeable, while pyroxylin powders vary according to their composition. However, from its origin it is in no wise different from the perfected powder of Vieille (although considerably different from the original form thereof), presenting instead of a mixture, from the chemical and mechanical standpoint, a homogeneous limiting mass of the composition $C_{30}H_{38}N_{12}O_{40}$, which is required in order that the powder may create upon combustion the maximum volume of vapor and gases. It is certain that henceforth pyroxylin powder will continue to approximate to the pyrocollodion until the two become identical. In brief, pyrocollodion represents the Russian limit of modification and improvement of the French pyroxylin powders, the development of which marked an epoch in ordnance progress, but which has not hitherto presented an invariable and constant relation of the elements entering into its composition. In this light pyrocollodion powder may well be styled Franco-Russian. Begun in France, it has been completed in Russia.

APPENDIX III

THE NITRATION OF COTTON

By M. Bruley

WITHIN recent years different varieties of nitro-cellulose which hitherto have possessed only very restricted uses have had their fields of application broadened, especially in their relation to the manu-facture of explosives.

Photographic collodions, celluloid, artificial silk, etc., have nitro-cellulose for their bases. On the other hand, besides gun-cotton, employed for military purposes, as for the charging of torpedoes and other similar appliances, nitro-cellulose enters into the com-position of various kinds of smokeless powders, gum-dynamites, cartridges for use in presence of fire-damp, etc.

Each of these applications demands, so to speak, a special variety of nitro-cellulose, and the government explosive-factories entrusted with their preparation, so far as relates to their use as explosives, have been gradually forced to meet requirements differing widely as to character.

For a long time the Moulin Blanc factory, which was established for the production of naval gun-cotton, had scarcely more to do than to produce gun-cotton of maximum nitration for military uses. For this the well-known mixture of three parts sulphuric acid by weight of 65.5 Baumé and one part by weight of nitric acid of 48 Baumé, has always been employed.

Since then the Moulin Blanc works and those at Angoulême, where the manufacture of gun-cotton was established in 1887, have had to produce other kinds of nitro-cellulose, which it became necessary to manufacture practically in a regular manner.

The theoretical researches of M. Vieille, described in his note of September 13, 1883, inserted in Vol. II of the "Mémorial des Poudres et Salpêtres" (p. 212 *et seq.*), classified different varieties of nitro-cellulose in the manner following, in accordance with the formulæ for their chemical composition:

		Vol. of Nitrogen Dioxide Disengaged per gram	
Cellulose endecanitrate	214	} gun-cottons.
" decanitrate	203	
" enneanitrate	190	} collodions.
" octonitrate	178	
" heptanitrate	162	
" hexanitrate	146	} friable cottons.
" pentanitrate	128	
" tetranitrate	108	

Gun-cotton, as well as friable cottons, are insoluble in a mixture of alcohol and sulphuric ether, while collodions, on the contrary, are soluble in such a mixture.

Indeed, it is hardly possible to isolate each one of

these varieties, and one always finds mixtures of two
or more neighboring varieties.

Thus in practice, the products obtained are classed,
not into cellulose endecanitrate, cellulose decanitrate,
etc., but into gun-cotton properly so-called, for which
the content of nitrogen is between 210 and 200 c.c.,
into superior and inferior collodions, with nitrogen
content ranging between 190 and 180 c.c. for the
former and from 180 to 170 for the latter; and friable
cottons.

Gun-cotton, properly so-called, is theoretically insoluble in ether-alcohol. In reality it always contains
small quantities of less highly nitrated soluble products.
Collodions deposit in this solvent an insoluble residue,
due to the presence of non-attacked cotton, or friable
cottons, or even more highly nitrated cottons.

It is for this reason that solubility in ether-alcohol
is determined the same time that nitration is estimated.

The different soluble collodions are distinguishable
from one another, moreover, by the greater or less
viscosity of the solution obtained. As this property
is one that may possess practical importance in the
employment of collodions, it appears useful to study
it simultaneously with the solubility and the content
of nitrogen.

A series of researches were undertaken at the Angoulême powder-works for the purpose of determining
the practical method of obtaining a chosen product
from the series of those just enumerated. These
researches do not claim to possess the scientific value
of those made in 1883 by M. Vieille upon the nitra-

tion of cotton. The resources at the powder-works laboratory, especially in relation to personnel, are too limited to justify the hope of rigorous precision for results obtained. But apart from their utility as a guide in the manufacture of a desired product, they seem to possess a certain interest in relation to the conditions controlling the nitration of cotton.

I. METHOD OF NITRATION AND MODE OF REPRESENTING RESULTS

M. Vieille in his researches in 1883 had employed two methods of nitration. In one he used mixtures containing only nitric acid and water. In the other he added to these bodies variable proportions of sulphuric acid.

The latter method has been alone employed in practice; it is the one exclusively used in the trials that constitute the object of the present work.

Apart from nitrous vapors, which are always present in appreciable but very feeble quantities, and foreign matters, which are never found in the acids employed except in negligable quantities, every mixture employed for dipping cotton for the production of any one of the various nitro-celluloses contains the three following elements: monohydrated sulphuric acid, H_2SO_4; monohydrated nitric acid, HNO_3; and water, H_2O.

If we desire to classify the infinite number of mixtures that may be obtained from all possible combinations of the three elements, in groups giving rise finally to products of the same kind, it is necessary to have recourse to a graphic method of representation of these mixtures.

In expressing the relations of the proportions of the two elements to the third, each mixture is defined by only two numbers. It is easy, then, by employing one of them as an abscissa and the other as an ordinate, to express by the ordinary system of rectangular coördinates any mixture determined by a single point.

The different mixtures giving rise to the same product will thus be grouped by zones, and a knowledge of these zones will facilitate the practical obtaining of a desired nitro-cellulose, whether new acids are employed to produce it or whether spent acids from a previous manufacture are employed for the purpose.

II. RESULTS OBTAINED BY M. VIEILLE

We shall reconsider, in the order of ideas just indicated, the results obtained by M. Vieille in 1883, and mentioned in the preceding note.

In all experiments under the second method, sulphuric acid of density 1.832 was employed, corresponding, according to the special tables, to a degree by areometer of 65.5 Baumé and to a percentage of water of about 8; and, upon the other hand, to nitric acid of density 1.316 which, if it be supposed free from all traces of. nitrous vapors, should mark 34.6 by the Baumé areometer and contain 50% of water.

Applying these figures to the volumetric proportions of each mixture given in the table on page 87, the following new table is formed:

No. of Ex- periment	Proportions of Components			Per cent. of Ni- trogen Dioxide in Product ob- tained	Observations
	H_2SO_4	HNO_3	H_2O		
1	100	13.1	21.7	195 9	
2	100	15.5	24.3	190.1	
3	100	19.5	28.2	184.6	
4	100	22.9	31.7	185.5	
5	100	26.0	34.8	182.3	Solubility
6	100	27.8	36.5	164.0	n o t deter-
7	100	30.0	38.6	166.7	mined
8	100	32.4	41.1	166.0	
9	100	35.4	44.1	141.2	
10	100	39.0	47.6	143.5	
11	100	41.0	49.8	133.2	
12	100	43.3	61.9	132.7	

Under the system of representation adopted, by which the proportions of the two other elements are expressed as ratios to 100 parts by weight of H_2SO_4, the figures of the preceding table may be graphically expressed as in Fig. 1, page 133.

All the points representing the mixtures employed lie upon 'the same straight line ab, since they are formed with the same nitric acid marking 34.6° by the Baumé areometer. This line is inclined at 45°, since the acid chosen contains as much water as mono-hydrated acid; it starts from the point a corresponding to eight per cent., there being exactly that much water in one hundred parts of the sulphuric acid to which the one hundred parts of the other components are expressed as ratios.

Outside of this line there exist an infinite number of other points corresponding to acid mixtures the action of which upon cotton was not studied by M. Vieille. By employing nitric acid of increasing strengths successively, along with sulphuric acid of 65.5° Baumé, mixtures will be obtained represented by points upon the lines *ac*, *ad*, etc., which start from the common point *a* and are more or less inclined according to the

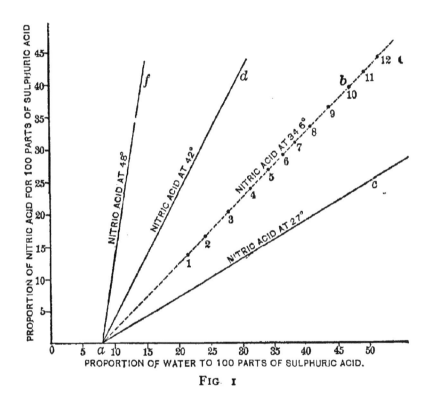

FIG. I

quantity of water in the acid employed. The practical limit is the line *af* corresponding to 48° Baumé, the strongest obtainable in current manufacture, and which contains about 10 per cent. water.

These are the regions left aside in previous studies, the exploration of which is now undertaken from the

standpoint of practical results to be obtained industri-
ally from the corresponding acid mixtures.

III. EXPERIMENTS IN NITRATION.   (FIRST SERIES)

In this first series of experiments the base material
was the chemically pure absorbent cotton employed in
pharmacy. - The acid mixtures were prepared direct
from the three principal elements, sulphuric acid, nitric
acid and water. For this purpose a carboy of sulphuric acid of 65.7° Baumé was drawn from current
supplies. On the other hand a certain quantity
of nitric acid of the highest possible strength had
been collected at the nitric-acid factory, and from this
nitrous vapors were completely expelled by passing
carbonic-acid gas through it for a number of hours at
a temperature of about 70° C. After expulsion of
fumes this acid marked 47.7° Baumé.

The selected sulphuric and nitric acids were kept in
carboys carefully sealed and provided with a com-
pressed-air emptying system, the air used being carefully freed from all traces of moisture. As all the experiments could not be carried on at the same time, it
was necessary to provide that the elements entering
into them should be always identical.

The water present in the acids was that shown by
the special table corresponding to their areometric degree, this quantity being checked by direct analysis,
and was 6.5 per cent. for the sulphuric and 10.5 per
cent. for the nitric acid.

The mixtures employed for the experiments were
determined by adding to the quantities of the two

acids taken the quantity of water necessary to bring the total weight up to 1.2 kilos. The percentage compositions were deduced from these weights and that of the water in the acid components.

Each mixture was divided into three lots of 400 grams each, of which two were employed for duplicate experiments and one was held in reserve.

The 400 grams of mixed acid were introduced into a large-mouthed flask provided with an air-tight stopper, and an equilibrium of temperature established; then the four grams of absorbent cotton were added and the flask violently shaken. Under these conditions nitration took place almost instantaneously, and it may be said that each fibre of cotton was instantly surrounded with 100 times its weight of liquid acid.

The flask was then corked and placed under a stream of water maintained at a constant temperature of from 18° to 19° C., which was that of dipping, the cotton remaining the whole time in the acid bath.

Two dippings were made for each mixture studied, one of them corresponding to reaction double in length of time to that of the other. The admitted durations of reaction were six, twelve, and twenty-four hours, according to the kind of nitro-cellulose that was supposed should be obtained.

It was not considered necessary to study reactions of longer duration, difficult to realize in practice. In certain cases it was deemed sufficient to control results by reconducting the experiment in a bath of the same composition, and allowing the reaction to continue for forty-eight and even up to sixty hours.

Twenty-five mixtures, corresponding pretty nearly to the whole region embraced by those obtainable in practice, were thus experimented with; that is to say, by maintaining as proportions of nitric acid and water expressed in ratios to one hundred parts of sulphuric acid by weight, from 10 to 60 per cent. of the former and from 10 to 45 per cent. of the latter.

In fact, for nitric acid below a certain limit, reactions became too slow. On the other hand, from a standpoint of economy, its proportion cannot be too much increased on account of its relatively high price. As to water, its lower limit is fixed by the strength of the strongest acids obtainable in current manufacture.

The twenty-five mixtures studied represent sufficiently well, then, the region that may be explored in practice; they are spaced apart regularly, so that by the examination of the products obtained, proper account may be taken of the phenomenon of nitration throughout the region explored.

The percentage of nitrogen in each of the products thus obtained was determined by Schloessing's method, described at the close of M. Vieille's paper above referred to. Solubility in ether-alcohol and viscosity in that medium were determined under the methods employed at the Angoulême powder-works and described at the end of the present paper.

The following table presents a resumé of all results obtained from the analysis of specimens produced in this first series of experiments:

| Number of Order of Mixtures | Composition of Mixtures | | | Results Obtained for a Duration of Reaction of | | | | | | | | |
| | Sulphuric Acid | Nitric Acid | Water | 6 Hours | | | 12 Hours | | | 24 Hours | | |
				Nitrogen Expressed as NO₂ in c.c.	Solu-bility in %	Viscosity s.	Nitrogen as NO₂ in c.c.	Solu-bility in %	Viscosity s.	Nitrogen as NO₂ in c.c.	Solu-bility in %	Viscosity s.
I	100	59.1	29.6	204.0	55.3		203.8	46.5		211.0	2.1	
II	"	49.1	24.3				211.0	2		211.6	1.5	
III	"	39.6	18.8				211.6	1.1		209.2	4.2	
IV	"	19.4	14.2				209.2	3.4		183.8	16.1	
V	"	9.7	14.3				173.4	17.8		179.2	94.8	22
VI	"	9.4	24.2				171.8	82.1				
VII	"	19.1	23.4	199.2	73.7		199.2	66.6	18			
VIII[1]	"	19.5	34.2									
IX	"	29.8	23.9	208.6	11.9		206.8	9.5				
X	"	39.0	29.8	192.4	98.5	128	193.4	97.6	145			
XI	"	58.9	38.5	178.4	96.6	67	179.2	95.6	69			
XII	"	49.2	34.1	186.8	96.9	81	187.0	96.0	80			
XIII	"	29.3	34.2	170.4	96.0	43	174.2	94.9	51			
XIV	"	39.9	38.4	169.4	93.1	61	170.4	96.9	57			
XV	"	49.7	43.2	157.6	73.8		157.6	85.6				
XVI	"	58.3	34.4	192.6	97.5	124	195.2	98.8	202			
XVII	"	48.5	29.7	200.4	97.4	256	201.8	94.2	322			
XVIII	"	48.2	39.1	173.4	96.1	80	174.8	96.5	66			
XIX	"	39.0	24.5	206.0	3.3		207.6	3.6				
XX	"	38.8	34.1	183.4	98.4	116	184.0	91.6	83			
XXI	"	29.3	19.0				210.0	1.5				
XXII	"	29.5	28.9	195.6	98.1	123	195.6	94.0	110	210.8	1.5	
XXIII	"	19.6	19.1				209.8	4.4		209.8	2.7	
XXIV	"	19.4	29.0	175.4	95.8	55	180.8	97.1	43	207.8	5.5	
XXV	"	14.9	18.7				207.8	6.6				

[1] Cotton dissolved in acid

Inspection of this table shows that mixtures in which the percentage of nitric acid is low, and notably mixtures V and VI, produce after twelve hours reaction an incompletely nitrated product. Even after twenty-four hours the nitration is not complete; a fact verified by certain complementary experiments for these latter. They will be discarded, then, as out of the category of practical mixtures.

The graphic representation of the other mixtures, by the method above indicated, is reproduced below (Fig. 2). By the side of each point representing one of them, the corresponding number is indicated in Roman numerals; and the principal qualities of the product taken from the preceding table are expressed in ordinary figures, the figures chosen for each reaction being those corresponding to the longest duration of reaction. The first number is the percentage of nitrogen; the second, the solubility; the third, when given, the viscosity.

If, as indicated at the beginning of this article, the products be divided into gun-cottons, collodions and friable cottons, overlooking certain small quantities of accompanying products that may be mingled with them, it will be seen that mixtures giving rise to products of the same kind may be grouped in quite distinct zones. The lines which limit these zones are nearly parallel to one another. They depart a little from the straight line and are slightly inclined to the co-ordinate axes; percentages of nitrogen and solubilities alone have served for tracing them. Viscosities, which refer to collodions only, are pre-

sented only as indicators, and are far from being the
same for all products in a given zone.

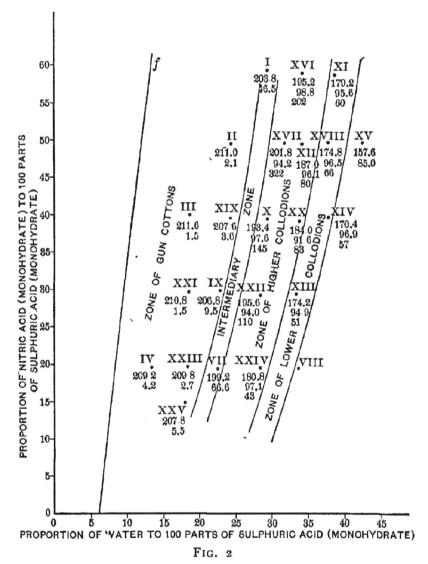

FIG. 2

Without being able to discover, in results obtained
for these viscosities, the expression of any well-defined law, it may be remarked, however, that they are

in general greater, according as the corresponding percentages of nitrogen themselves are greater. Thus it is to be remarked that the mean viscosity for the zone of lower collodions is 65^s, while for the higher collodions the mean attains 140^s.

IV. EXPERIMENTS IN NITRATION. (SECOND SERIES)

The preceding results were obtained, as indicated, with pure wadded cotton. In general this is not the base material employed, but spinning waste, bleached and freed from grease, which costs less. The fibres of the cotton are more or less twisted and entangled, and, notwithstanding the effects of carding, there always remain at the time of dipping small agglomerations, into which the acid penetrates with difficulty. In order to estimate the influence of the base material employed upon results obtained, a second series of trials were undertaken under conditions similar to those of the first series, except that the refuse cotton from current manufacture was substituted for the absorbent wadding. During this series of experiments the temperature was maintained during the whole time of the dipping at about from 7° to 8° C. The acid mixtures were prepared as indicated above. The sulphuric acid employed marked 65 8° Baumé, and contained only 5 per cent. of water. The nitric acid, freed from nitrous vapors, marked 47.1° Baumé and contained 15 per cent. of water. The per cent. composition of each of the twenty-five mixtures employed was calculated on the basis of these figures, and verified for a certain number of cases by direct analysis. As above stated, 4 grams of cotton were immersed in 400 grams of acid. The absorption of the cotton by the liquid proceeded as rapidly as with the wadding.

The table on page 142 presents the results obtained in the second series of experiments.

More clearly than in the preceding series, it is to be remarked that for a certain number of mixtures, especially for those in which the relative proportion of nitric acid is low, prolongation of the reaction increases the percentage of nitration. We shall discard mixtures V and VI as heretofore, since the reaction, to be complete, would have to be prolonged too far.

Figure 3 (page 143) represents graphically the results of the second series of experiments.

As in the preceding series, different mixtures, producing products of the same kind are grouped in zones, and these zones are sensibly of the same form as those of Fig. 2; still again, but this time perhaps a little less clearly, however, the viscosity of the collodions appears to increase with the percentage of nitration.

V. EXPERIMENTS IN NITRATION. (THIRD SERIES)

A third series of dippings was finally undertaken, the conditions of which were practically identical with those obtaining in practice. Bleached English

Number of Order of Mixtures	Composition of Mixtures			Results obtained for a Duration of Reaction of								
	Sulphuric Acid	Nitric Acid	Water	6 Hours			12 Hours			24 Hours		
				Nitrogen Expressed as NO_3 in c.c.	Solubility in %	Viscosity s.	Nitrogen as NO_3 in c.c.	Solubility in %	Viscosity s.	Nitrogen as NO_3 in c.c.	Solubility in %	Viscosity s.
I	100	55.2	30.7	194.8	97.3	105	194.2	97.2	129			
II	"	45.9	24.7	202.2	16.0		205.0	7.7				
III	"	37.1	18.8				209.6	2.0		211.0	1.2	
IV	"	18.2	13.6				204.8	2.2		208.8	1.7	
V	"	9.2	12.9				121.4	20.8		141.0	18.5	
VI	"	8.8	22.8	188.8	90.4		123.4	59.5		129.9	54.7	
VII	"	18.0	22.5				193.2	92.0				
VIII[1]	"	18.3	33.2				"	"				
IX	"	28.0	23.5	197.8	83.5		200.4	80.4				
X	"	36.6	29.8	186.6	96.1	141	187.4	96.5	92			
XI	"	54.9	39.2	162.2	90.5		166.8	92.3				
XII	"	46.0	34.4	177.2	96.1	60	178.2	94.1	72			
XIII	"	27.4	33.7	153.4	36.1		154.6	41.2				
XIV	"	37.2	38.2	148.4	19.1		148.2	25.4				
XV	"	46.4	44.3	141.2	2.5		141.2	2.9				
XVI	"	54.6	35.6	178.0	96.9	78	173.6	97.2	70			
XVII	"	45.3	30.2	189.8	97.7	91	190.6	98.4	88			
XVIII	"	44.9	39.2	151.4	26.9		155.2	24.1				
XIX	"	36.6	24.7	198.0	92.9		199.6	81.9				
XX	"	.36.2	34.4	166.8	86.3		178.8	93.2				
XXI	"	27.4	18.5	209.0	4.8		210.0	3.9				
XXII	"	27.6	28.4	184.4	95.2	37	187.4	96.2				
XXIII	"	18.4	18.2				204.4	8.5				
XXIV	"	18.1	27.8	167.6	92.2	46	169.6	96.5	69	207.8	7.0	
XXV	"	13.9	17.6				196.6	24.5	82	198.6	11.0	

1 Cotton dissolved in acid

spun-cotton waste from the powder-factory suppʌies, was employed as the base material. This was dipped in different acid mixtures formed, as indicated above,

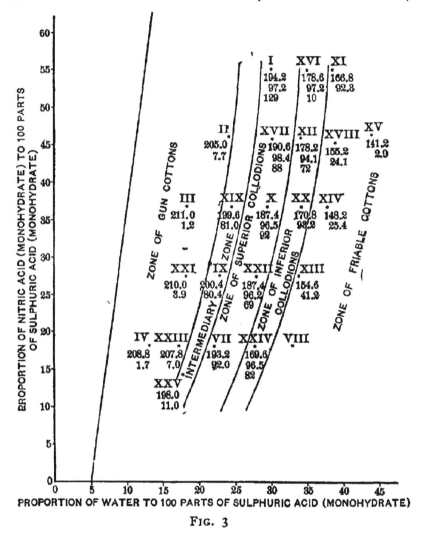

FIG. 3

from distilled water and the sulphuric and nitric acids of which part had been employed in the preceding experiments. The proportions for dippings were always the same; 4 grams of cotton to 400 grams of mixed acids; but the duration of immersion of the cotton in the acid bath was reduced to eight minutes. After such immersion at a constant temperature (12° to 13° C. approx.) the cotton was removed, drained, lightly pressed, and placed in an earthenware crock in which the reaction completed itself, the pot being placed in a stream of water at the current temperature.

The results from this third series of experiments are given in the table on page 145.

These results may be expressed graphically in the manner shown in Fig. 4, page 146, neglecting mixtures V, VI and XXV, which only produced partially nitrated products.

Still again, the products obtained allow the mixtures to be grouped into zones analogous to those resulting from the two other series of experiments. In each of these zones viscosities are variable and appear not to follow a well-defined law, although high viscosities accompany the highest percentages of nitrogen.

VI. VARIOUS EXPERIMENTS

The experiments of which a resumé has just been given exhibit the influence of acid mixtures upon the products obtained. Here, indeed, lies the principal element entering into the whole manufacture of nitro-cellulose. But other, secondary causes may equally influence final results, and it has appeared useful to

Number of Order of Mixtures	Composition of Mixtures			General Results from a Duration of Reaction of								
	Sulphuric Acid	Nitric Acid	Water	6 Hours			12 Hours			24 Hours		
				Nitrogen Expressed as NO₂ in c.c.	Solubility in %	Viscosity s	Nitrogen as NO₂ in c.c.	Solubility in %	Viscosity s	Nitrogen as NO₂ in c.c.	Solubility in %	Viscosity s
I	100	55.0	28.8	196.2	99.0	195	197.2	97.0	206			
II	"	45.9	24.3	205.0	52.9		205.8	52.9				
III	"	37.2	18.3	206.8	2.6		209.6	2.4				
IV	"	18.3	13.1	295.8	5.2		203.2	5.2		205.2	2.5	
V	"	9.1	10.9	122.6	19.8		128.2	20.1		134.0	14.2	
VI	"	9.4	21.3	143.0	19.1		142.8	19.4		147.8	21.9	
VII	"	18.0	20.8	183.4	89.7	52	182.0	90.9	45			
VIII¹	"	17.6	33.2				"	"				
IX	"	28.8	22.0	196.2	95.4	117	196.2	97.2	108			
X	"	37.5	29.3	184.6	96.3	86	186.2	95.8	90			
XI	"	54.9	37.8	164.4	87.5	53	164.6	94.4	41	172.6	95.3	45
XII	"	47.0	34.6	171.6	92.8		172.6	96.8	40	177.0	96.4	74
XIII	"	27.5	33.3	153.4	47.0		154.2	61.8		157.2	66.0	
XIV	"	37.3	38.0	144.4	16.0		146.2	14.0		146.8	10.8	
XV	"	47.6	45.4	121.6	1.4		123.6	1.5		142.8	1.9	
XVI	"	54.1	34.5	174.2	94.8	33	178.6	96.5	45	178.2	91.6	151
XVII	"	45.1	28.3	185.0	96.9	40	186.2	97.8	51			
XVIII	"	45.4	38.4	155.2	26.0		155.6	39.8		152.8	21.8	
XIX	"	36.5	23.7	197.6	92.2	178	199.8	91.3	122			
XX	"	36.4	33.5	163.4	86.4	58	163.4	81.8	59	164.6	80.8	71
XXI	"	27.7	18.4	207.8	5.4		208.8	3.3				
XXII	"	27.8	28.5	180.4	94.5	97	182.0	96.2	107	180.2	95.7	72
XXIII	"	18.3	18.1	193.2	20.0		201.6	21.9				
XXIV	"	18.1	28.0	160.4	65.1		162.4	65.7		162.6	77.4	
XXV	"	13.9	17.6	168.0	26.2		175.0	28.0		187.0	6.2	

¹ Cotton dissolved in acid

study them also. Among these causes, duration of
reaction has been briefly touched upon already, as
well as the nature of the base material. To these must

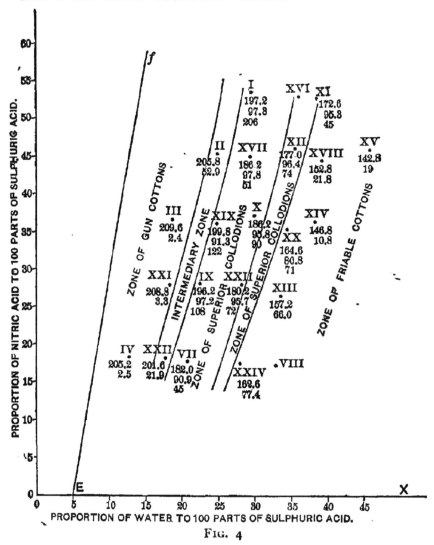

FIG. 4

be added temperature during dipping and reaction, as
well as the later effect of the manipulations that nitrated cotton may undergo after the operation of

dipping. These different effects will be examined successively.

Base materials.—Cotton wadding nitrates more readily than spun-cotton waste, which nitrates with the greater difficulty the more it is tangled, the coarser its threads, and the more knots it contains. On the other hand, it equally appears that the previous preparation of the waste destined for dipping exercises a very sensible influence upon the viscosity of the collodions obtained. Thus it is that two cottons of absolutely different origin, submitted under identical conditions to the action of a common acid mixture, produce collodions possessing the same mean percentage of nitrogen, but with viscosities varying from what they ordinarily are to double this.

Duration of reaction.—The appended table, in which two or three durations of reaction correspond to each mixture, shows that for a same final product, the reaction should be the more prolonged the lower the proportion of nitric acid in the mixture.

Some experiments were made to follow more closely the progress of the reaction; a resumé of them is presented in the following table. These experiments refer to three acid mixtures from the first series, the numbers of which are recalled in reference to results obtained; the conditions of dipping and reaction are those of this series; the temperature of the reaction was about 20° C. approximately:

Duration of Reaction	Mixture XIII		Mixture XVI		Mixture XXI	
	Nitrogen c.c NO$_2$	Solubility in %	Nitrogen c.c. NO$_2$	Solubility in %	Nitrogen c.c. NO$_2$	Solubility in %
1 hour	165.8	91.7	186.8	94 9	206.4	10.9
2 hours	166 8	95.5	189	95 0	209.4	8.3
4 "	167 8	93 0	191.8	96 2	209.2	6.8
6 "	167 8	94.8	198	94.1	210 2	6.7
8 "	166.8	95.4	191 8	96.7	210 2	5.6
12 "					210 8	7.4
24 "	166.8	98.1	194	96.6	210.6	10.6

These experiments comprise the three principal types of nitro-cellulose studied; superior and inferior collodions and gun-cotton. They show that for the two former a maximum of nitration is hardly obtained before the end of two hours of reaction; for gun-cotton, on the other hand, from eight to ten hours are required. If the reaction be prolonged beyond these limits, the solubility has a tendency to increase. In these experiments viscosity could not be measured; but the preceding tables seem to show that no relation exists between it and duration of reaction.

Temperatures of dipping and reaction.—A certain number of dippings were made under conditions identical with those of the second series of experiments, at the three very different temperatures of 1°, 12° and 25° C. These temperatures were maintained throughout the whole duration of the reaction.

Results obtained are grouped in the following table:

No. of Acid Mixtures	Duration of Reaction	Temperature during Dipping and Reaction								
		1° C.			12° C.			25° C.		
	hrs.	Nitrogen as NO_2 in c.c.	Solubility in %	Viscosity s.	Nitrogen as NO_2 in c.c.	Solubility in %	Viscosity s.	Nitrogen as NO_2 in c.c.	Solubility in %	Viscosity s.
I	6	190.0	95.9	180	191.8	97.8	104	193.2	97.7	56
III	12	208.2	1.5		207.4	1.7		207.8	1.0	
VI	12	201.6	4.4		205.4	4.4		207.6	3.6	
VII	6	177.6	84.9	22	189.0	92.9	60	193.2	97.7	36
X	6	178.8	95.1	145	185.4	96.8	72	184.4	96.2	61
XII	6	167.2	78.9	38	172.0	92.9	36	172.0	96.1	27

Other experiments were made to the same end with wadded cotton under the conditions of the first series. The results were as follows:

No. of Acid Mixtures	Duration of Reaction	Temperature during Dipping and Reaction								
		2° C.			15° C.			26° C.		
	hrs.	Nitrogen NO_2 in c.c	Solubility in %	Viscosity s.	Nitrogen NO_2 in c.c.	Solubility in %	Viscosity s.	Nitrogen NO_2 in c.c.	Solubility in %	Viscosity s.
XII	6	183.2	96.5		186.8	96.7		189.2	97.3	
"	12	183.2	97.4		186.8	95.1		188.2	94.4	
XIII	6	167.4	93.8		169.0	93.2	'	173.4	93.0	
"	12	165.6	90.7		166.0	94.5		168.6	94.1	
XV	6	188.8	96.5	43	192.8	98.1	48	194.0	98.3	22
"	12	188.8	97.4	37	191.8	97.0	26	193.6	98.1	20
XXI	12	208.8	8.9		209.2	9.2		208.6	7.1	
"	24	209.8	6.7		209.2	7.0		208.4	8.4	

These experiments seemed to show that, so far as collodions were concerned, increase of temperature during dipping and reaction increases the percentage of nitrogen and the solubility, but sensibly diminishes

the viscosity. In other words, a low temperature retards the reaction. In what relates to gun-cottons,
the influence manifests itself less distinctly; it is admitted, however, that at high temperatures the solubility has a tendency to increase.

Subsequent manipulations.—The different celluloses are submitted before use to a number of
manipulations; first to washings, which are necessary
to remove the last traces of acidity, and for certain
ones to pulping, which serves to facilitate subsequent
operations.

Washing is effected by a more or less prolonged
boiling, either in pure water or in an alkaline solution; the pulping by beating-engines similar to the apparatus employed in the manufacture of paper.

These operations, which are absolutely mechanical,
have no influence upon the chemical composition of
the final product, and therefore upon the percentage
of nitrogen; but it is different for solubility and viscosity, which are purely physical properties.

Experiments were made with the view of ascertaining how various kinds of nitro-celluloses acted during
these operations. Results are grouped in the tables
on page 151.

These various experiments were made with quite
large quantities of gun-cotton, consequently more or
less homogeneous, so that taking of samples should
suffice to explain certain anomalies to be noticed in
the progress of phenomena observed. From the
figures in the preceding tables it may be concluded,
on the one hand, that the two operations of washing

I. EFFECT OF WASHING ON GUN-COTTON

Qualities of Product after a Total Period of Boiling of

20 Hours		60 Hours		100 Hours		140 Hours		220 Hours		260 Hours	
Nitrogen NO₂ in c.c.	Solubility in %	Nitrogen NO₂ in c.c.	Solubility in %	Nitrogen NO₂ in c.c.	Solubility in %	Nitrogen NO₂ in c.c.	Solubility in %	Nitrogen NO₂ in c.c.	Solubility in %	Nitrogen NO₂ in c.c.	Solubility in %
207.2	5.2	206.4	11.3	206.6	10.9	206.0	14.8	206.4	21.2	206.2	22.4

II. EFFECT OF PULPING ON GUN-COTTON

Quality of Product after a Duration of Pulping of

Before Pulping		1 Hour		2 Hours		6 Hours		8 Hours		12 Hours	
Nitrogen NO₂ in c.c.	Solubility in %	Nitrogen NO₂ in c.c.	Solubility in %	Nitrogen NO₂ in c.c.	Solubility in %	Nitrogen NO₂ in c.c.	Solubility in %	Nitrogen NO₂ in c.c.	Solubility in %	Nitrogen NO₂ in c.c.	Solubility in %
204.8	12.8	204.8	17.6	204.8	18.6	204.0	20.0	204.0	19.7	203.6	22.4

III. EFFECT OF WASHING AND PULPING ON THE VISCOSITY OF COLLODIONS

Viscosity of Products obtained after a Duration of Boiling of

Number of Specimens	10 Hours s.	14 Hours s.	18 Hours s.	24 Hours s.	32 Hours s.	40 Hours s.	48 Hours s.	60 Hours s.	Before Pulping s.	After Pulping s.
1	703	454	424	389	279	254	237	140	109	82
2	815	815	865	780	450	380	272		228	117
3	144	133	115	114	92	83	75		92	50
4	136	118	128	123	80	111	74		89	53

in warm water and pulping have the effect of increasing the solubility of gun-cottons; on the other hand, that these two operations diminish to a marked degree the viscosity of the collodions.

VII. RESUMÉ AND CONCLUSIONS

As already stated, the results of the experiments just described complete in a certain sense those obtained by M. Vieille in 1883, since they relate to a series of mixtures that had not been studied up to this time.

Apart from the theoretical interest they may possess, they also possess a practical utility.

When it is desired to produce a certain definite nitro-cellulose, the first thing to determine upon is the composition of the dipping mixture to be employed. Heretofore, the proportions of the different elements, whether new or spent acids, were calculated somewhat arbitrarily. The experiments, of which a resumé has just been given, permit a more methodical procedure in such a case.

These are only laboratory experiments, it is true; and in practice a thousand causes, more or less well understood, arise to influence final results. Some supplementary experiments have been made to ascertain how these known causes tend; but it would be rash to assert that it would be possible, on the strength of the data afforded by these experiments, to obtain with certainty a product of which all the qualities were predetermined.

However, the great similarity of the results obtained in the three series of experiments, each of which approaches more nearly than the preceding to conditions obtaining in practice, justifies the belief that, although no one of them may enable us to calculate the proportions of a mixture capable of producing a certain product, nevertheless, the general trend of the phenomenon of nitration is that indicated by the position and relative importance of the different zones above referred to.

The knowledge of this progress in the phenomenon of nitration permits us, then, after a preliminary trial, which, besides, is not undertaken by chance, to modify, if necessary, the proportions of the mixture first taken, in such a way as to arrive at a desired end.

Different considerations serve as guides in the preparation of the preliminary mixture. While still keeping within the zone corresponding to the product desired, the relative proportions of nitric acid and water may be varied between quite wide limits. It is desirable, from the standpoint of economy, to diminish the quantity of the most expensive element; that is to say, the nitric acid; in certain cases, however, to develop certain qualities in the final product, we may be led to increase it. Finally, if spent acids of known composition are to be employed, one mixture may be found more advantageous than another, according to the relative quantities of acids to be taken.

The acids used, nitric acid or spent acids, always contain nitrous vapors to a small extent. These nitrous vapors may, if present in sensible quantity, falsify conditions upon which it was thought reliance could be placed, and this fact must be borne in mind in calculating the trial mixture. But in practice the proportion does not exceed from 1 to 2 per cent., and within these limits it may be admitted that the presence of nitrous vapors does not change results sensibly.

It is necessary, besides, to bear in mind that on account of the reaction that takes place in the dipping-vats, and which produces water, the proportions of sulphuric acid, nitric acid and water in the vats are no longer the same as those of the original mixture. These alone are the conditions which affect the degree of nitration and are determined beforehand according to the considerations just indicated. The others, which must also be known, since they serve in preparing the mixtures properly so-called, are easily deduced by means of corrections, which depend upon the size of the vats, the relative weight of cotton employed each time, etc., etc.; and they are determined in practice, by analysis, before and after dipping, of a certain number of mixtures most commonly employed.

When the formula for a mixture permitting desired results to be obtained is thus found, the choice of raw material to be dipped is also to be thought of, as well as temperature of dipping, duration and temperature of the reaction, etc., etc.

Here also, the experiments recalled above may serve as a guide to results to be obtained.

There always exist sensible differences between the industrial manufacture of a product and the laboratory process which serves as a basis for it. A thousand causes, varying from day to day, arise to modify the qualities of the final product. At first one proceeds only by guess-work; it is only in the end, as the result of the processes followed with method and perseverance, that one becomes able to define with exactness the effect produced by each one of a number of stated modifications.

With this line of thought a number of experiments were made at the Angoulême laboratory upon the production of nitro-celluloses. Much still remains to be done, but the results obtained already permit a more methodical procedure than in the past.

APPENDIX IV

THE DEVELOPMENT OF SMOKELESS POWDER *

By Lieutenant JOHN B. BERNADOU, U. S. Navy

THE systematic development of improved ballistic properties from progressive explosives constitutes one of the most important ordnance problems of the present day. The idea is beginning to gain ground among us that hereafter we must look to the powder, as well as to the gun, in our efforts to increase the rapidity of flight and the penetrative power of projectiles; that we must consider the source of energy at our disposal conjointly with the apparatus whose function it is to convert that energy into useful work.

So long as the art of powder-making remained at a standstill—as it practically did for several centuries —while the practices of alchemy, rather than the principles of chemistry, may be said to have controlled the manufacture of all explosives, the best that could be done was to follow the progress of mechanics in efforts to effect ordnance improvement; guns were built and powders were found to fire from them. To-

---

* Abstract of lecture delivered before the U. S. Naval War College, July 20, 1897.

day, however, not only is the composition of powder undergoing modification, but new explosive compounds, the development of which is based upon chemical discovery, are coming into general use; the results of investigations into the chemical and physical properties of explosives, systematized and coordinated by the methods of mathematical analysis, have so increased our knowledge of ballistics, that designers of ordnance are forced to accept new conditions as factors of prime importance in the attainment of ballistic effect.

For purposes of comparison, the old forms of powder, such as black gunpowder, may be regarded as imperfect mechanical mixtures of particles of the materials of which the powder is composed; the new explosives, as very intimate mixtures of the atoms of those elements from the union of which into molecules the substance of the explosive is formed. When the old powder is employed as a fine dust, it burns with great speed and violence; when agglomerated into grains* it burns in a slow, progressive manner. If the grains of the old powders become disintegrated before they are completely consumed, through effects of heat and gas pressure developed in the bore of the gun, the grains crumble away; pressures become violent and regular progressive combustion ceases to obtain. Similar, but not identical, conditions exist for the new explosives. In the form of dust they burn with

---

* By " grain " is to be understood any regular form, flat strips, rods, cubes, etc.

exceeding rapidity and great violence; when all the particles are decomposed simultaneously, they detonate; by building them up into dense grains they *may* be made, under favorable conditions, to burn progressively.

It was obvious from the start that many advantages were to be obtained by the substitution of the new explosives for the old as progressive powders. The former burned up completely, leaving no residue. Many of them made no smoke. Other conditions being equal, these two qualities alone would have been sufficient to justify their general adoption. But other conditions were not equal. Up to a few years ago the fact remained that no positive, certain means of making nitro-explosives burn progressively had been found. All known precautions could be observed in the preparation; they could be built up into dense grains with the greatest possible care; yet, every now and then a charge of the powder would detonate; that is, instead of burning progressively, in accordance with the finished form of its grains, it would burn as the dust from which the grains were built up. A gun would be shattered, perhaps a life or two lost, and then all confidence in the new material would disappear, the chosen line of development would be abandoned; no fundamental facts would be left unchallenged to anchor new hopes upon.

Until some way could be found, then, of firing a nitro-compound from a gun with positive assurance that detonation would not occur, there could be no change from the old powders to the new. This assurance was, however, obtained by the discovery that nitro-cellulose, colloided and formed into grains of regular size, would in all cases, if ignited in a closed space, burn away in a progressive manner, at a rate proportional to the form and dimensions of the grains and to the conditions of their confinement. Two proofs made the fact certain that colloids would not detonate; first, that the grains of colloid powders which were shot out of the gun without being completely consumed, preserved the original shapes, in reduced dimensions, of the grains of which the powder charge was primarily composed; second, that not tens, nor hundreds, but thousands of rounds of colloid powders, fired in guns or exploded in closed vessels, developed in every case pressures that could be shown to correspond rationally, in accordance with the theory of progressive combustion, to size and form of grains and to dimensions of gun-chamber or explosion-bomb. To make these facts certain, pressures were carried up beyond the 33,000-lb. limit allowed for cannon; and in explosion-bombs to well beyond 100,000 lbs. per square inch.

Now, as the only certain means yet found of avoiding detonation and of assuring progressive combustion is through the colloiding of nitro-cellulose, and as nitro-cellulose alone can be colloided, it follows that we are definitely limited in our choice of material for progressive powders to a certain preparation of nitro-cellulose. It is true that a number of substances, such as nitro-glycerin and nitrates of metallic bases, may be distributed in minute particles throughout the body of the colloid, and that immunity from simultaneous detonation may be secured for the particles so distributed; but they all remain uncombined in the colloid—the nitrates, as the sand or minute shells in the body of a sponge; the nitro-glycerin, as the water in the pores of the sponge. It is desired to emphasize by this comparison the fact that all the new powders, without exception, must be built up from some form of colloid nitro-cellulose, whether they contain other ingredients or not. Thus, in the case of those powders containing nitro-glycerin we may reduce the percentage of nitro-glycerin to zero; that is, we may eliminate it. If we were to remove the colloid nitro-cellulose from such a powder we would have remaining nitro-glycerin, which would detonate in the gun upon the attempt to fire.

Nitro-cellulose, which is usually prepared by dipping cotton into nitric acid, possesses a property which the cotton, before dipping into acid, does not, i.e., of dissolving in a number of substances. One of these is acetone, a volatile fluid, with a characteristic pungent and aromatic odor, somewhat suggesting common alcohol in appearance and properties. Another solvent for a different kind of nitro-cellulose is a mixture of ether and alcohol. If the clear liquids which constitute the solutions in these substances be evaporated, there will be obtained, not the nitrated cotton, in its original fibrous form, but first, a syrupy liquid, then a jelly, and finally, as dryness is approached, a solid translucent mass, varying in color according to the variety of nitro-cellulose from which it is prepared, from a straw-yellow to a chocolate-brown, and generally suggesting, in its various forms, tortoise-shell. To such a substance the appellation *colloid*, from its glue-like consistency, has been applied.

The general name for the material produced by steeping cellulose into nitric acid is nitro-cellulose. One of its common forms is gun-cotton. Chemists are well aware that there are many different kinds of nitro-cellulose, but just how many there are no one has as yet even been able to predict, the exact composition of cellulose and of its nitro-derivatives remaining among the yet unsolved mysteries of nature. Three forms were originally assigned to it, the mono-, di- and tri-, just as there were the three forms of mono-, di- and trinitro-glycerin. A later investigator (Eder) succeeded in proving the existence of six. The authority of to-day upon the subject, whose views are now generally accepted (Vieille), has formulated eight. Now, just as there are many varieties of nitro-cellulose, so there are many varieties of colloids. The nitro-celluloses themselves all look alike; in their common pulped form they suggest fine white flour. They can be distinguished from one another with ease by the readiness with which some of them go into solution in certain solvents, while others remain undissolved in these solvents like so much sand. The fact that they possess such different properties is accounted for in practice by proven differences in

chemical composition. It suffices here to state that
there are a number of different varieties of the substance which form a number of different colloids.
The question of composition will be considered later
in relation to the gases resulting from the combustion of nitro-compounds.

We are familiar with the kind of nitro-cellulose
used for detonating purposes—gun-cotton. We are
also familiar with a form of colloid in common use to-
day as a material. I refer here to celluloid, now very
generally employed for the manufacture of a great
number of useful articles. The nitro-cellulose from
which celluloid is prepared may be made by steeping cotton in weak acids, and is rather a combustible
than an explosive; it is a very different substance
from the high explosive, gun-cotton, which is prepared from cotton by the use of strong acids. One solvent used to make celluloid is a mixture of ether and
alcohol; the same solvent has no effect upon gun-cotton, to dissolve which acetone must be used. We
have, then, two different types of colloid to start
with—celluloid (formed from weakly nitrated cellulose by the use of ether-alcohol), and the acetone colloid of gun-cotton. It may be stated here that these
two types of colloids represent all that is important
in relation to colloid material for the manufacture of
smokeless powder, as the matter has been understood
up to a very recent date. The various colloids of the
eight varieties of gun-cotton above referred to range
themselves under one or the other of these two types.
We thus have two classes of colloid to experiment

with, as gunpowder, and all the information we possess in relation to them is the fact that, however they may burn in the gun, yet they will not detonate.

Suppose that a number of rounds of powder are prepared from the two colloids, how will they act when fired from a gun of a given calibre? Let us assume that we have at our disposal the instruments commonly employed for the measurement of muzzle velocities and of bore-pressures, the chronograph and pressure gauges; we will then have, as a basis of comparison, first, the ratios V/P of velocities to pressures*; second, our personal observations of other phenomena attending explosion.

Actual practice shows that the best results obtained for the two powders in a given gun, by varying weights of charge and dimensions of grain, would be about as follows:

Gun-cotton-acetone colloid .... $V/P = 2100/15-19$;

Celluloid nitro-cotton † colloided with } $V/P = 2100/16$.
    ether-alcohol.................... }

Inspection of the results shows the existence of a pressure-range of from fifteen to nineteen tons for the acetone powder; this means that while no detonation would occur, yet that pressures would jump between certain limits. Such a phenomenon is often observed in the tests of brown powders for heavy

---

* A convenient expression for comparing, in a given gun, the ballistic properties of different progressive powders,—V representing velocities in foot-seconds, and P, pressures in tons per square inch.

† Commonly called "soluble nitro-cellulose."

guns. A powder of this character would be unsuitable for general use by reason of pressure irregularity.

Upon firing the celluloid powder another and perhaps worse inconvenience would be met with. Considerable smoke would be developed and the interior of the bore would be found lined, after each round, with a heavy coating of soot, which, after one or two shots had been fired and the gun had become heated, would ignite after each succeeding round upon ingress of fresh air on opening of the breech, thereby producing flaming at breech and muzzle.

Obviously, as gunpowder, neither the one nor the other form of colloid is suitable. If they are to be employed they must be improved. Irregularity in pressures from the gun-cotton-acetone colloid is due to brittleness; if we are to use this material we must devise some means of toughening it. The celluloid does not contain enough oxygen to consume its substance into gases; to use the latter we must put more oxygen into it.

The original phases of the colloid powder question thus present themselves. Neither the one nor the other form of colloid proving suitable for direct manufacture into powder, people began to try to improve them by combining them, or by adding foreign substances to them. It was well understood that no form of gun-cotton, however highly nitrated, contained enough oxygen to effect its own complete combustion—the conversion of its carbon into the higher oxide of carbon, CO_2. The first idea of the experimenter was to add enough oxygen to the nitro-cellulose to thus complete its combustion, and this unfortunate attempt led to many years' delay in the development of smokeless powder. It started investigators off upon a wrong track; complete combustion was one thing, and the work necessary to develop highest velocity with lowest bore-pressure, another.

With the purpose, then, of improving ballistic qualities of powders by causing them to consume completely and to develop regular pressures, experimenters in different countries began to try the effect of introducing into the colloid various foreign substances,—generally, oxidizing agents, such as nitrates of metallic bases; sometimes, when the mixtures became too violent in their action, a substance rich in carbon, called a deterrent, was added. Such work was a good deal like groping in the dark. There was no method in it. But there was one great incentive to keeping it up, viz., the fact thereby established that the addition of these nitrates to the colloids actually increased the velocity developed for a given bore-pressure, whatever the inconveniences attendant upon the employment of these mixtures as powders may have been.*

To establish a comparison between the ballistic efficiencies of the two types of pure colloids above

---

* The increase in muzzle velocities for a given bore-pressure to be attained by incorporating certain quantities of metallic nitrates, nitro-glycerin, etc., into the body of the colloid, constitutes a special phase of development of progressive powders, which will be discussed in a subsequent paper.

cited, and of certain compound colloid powders into the substance of which metallic nitrates or other oxygen-carriers are incorporated, the tabular record of performances of powders of these classes is submitted on page 167. Note is made therein of objectionable features developed for each of the explosives named.

Referring to the table we find powders A and B with properties as already described. The K, BN, and cordite all make good ballistic showings, giving velocities greater by about 300 ft. sec. for a developed pressure than the former.

The last line of the table shows that each of the powders possesses certain unfavorable qualities which militate against its adoption for service use. The gun-cotton acetone colloid develops irregular pressures; the ether-alcohol colloid of soluble nitrocellulose deposits soot; the K and BN produce some smoke and bore-deposit. Cordite contains a volatile liquid, nitro-glycerin, which develops great heat upon combustion. Now the development of highest velocity at lowest pressure is most important, even if obtained at the expense of the production of certain partially unfavorable conditions; but there was a further incentive to progress at this stage of development—the fact there had been found a form of pure colloid, unadulterated by admixture with other substances, which, while developing high velocities at moderate pressures, possessed the full round of good qualities necessary in a service powder.

The end sought for in the development of gunpowder is the attainment of the capability of deliver-

TABLE I

A	B	C	D	E
Acetone, gun-cotton, pure colloid	Ether-alcohol, soluble nitro-cellulose, pure colloid	K (Primitive type, United States.) Blend of nitro-celluloses colloided in acetone, with metallic nitrates added	BN (France, commercial.) Blend of nitro-celluloses colloided in ether-alcohol, with metallic nitrates added	Cordite (Great Britain.) Nitro-cellulose, colloided in acetone with nitro-glycerin added
$V/P = \dfrac{2100}{15 \text{ to } 19}$	$V/P = \dfrac{2100}{16}$	$V/P = \dfrac{2400}{15}$	$V/P = \dfrac{2400}{15}$	$V/P = \dfrac{2400}{15}$
Irregular pressures	Deposits soot	Some smoke and bore deposit	Some smoke and bore deposit	Erosion; doubtful keeping quality; some smoke

ing most accurately in a given interval of time the
greatest number of most powerful blows; this result
to be effected with minimum risk to gunners and with
least possible injury to gun. Hereby is implied the
fulfilment of a number of important independent
conditions, no one of which may be overlooked in the
effort to successfully accomplish the object sought.
These conditions correspond to qualities possessed
by a powder, and may be given, with their opposites,
a general grouping under headings as follows:

TABLE II

QUALITIES OF POWDERS

	1	2	3	4	5
Positive {	Non-liability to detonation	Devel'pment of minimum heat	Formation of minimum residue	Good keeping quali- ties	Maximum propulsive effect
Negative {	Detonation	Erosion	Smoke and bore-deposit	Decomposi- tion	Low value of V/P

The first condition is of paramount importance
and limits us to the employment of a colloid material.
The second represents the fact that the greater the
heat developed the greater the wearing away of the
inner surface of the bore. The third requirement
means obviation of bore-deposit, which operates to
reduce rapidity of fire by necessitating more or less
frequent sponging, and to diminish accuracy of practice through the formation of smoke. The fourth requirement, stability, is all-important, when we remember that the ship must carry safely her store of
powder for at least a cruise, and for the reason that

when powders begin to decompose they lose their homogeneity and crumble—which means an end to regular-pressure development.

Let us now take up requirement fifth—the attainment of maximum propulsive effect—and see what it leads to. What causes the expulsion of the projectile from the gun? The expansion of powder-gases. What limits our employment of the expansive force of these gases? The attainment of the limiting bore-pressure, this limit being commonly set at fifteen tons per square inch. What represents the greatest amount of work in the form of velocity? The greatest amount of gas-expansion in the gun behind the projectile.

We desire, then, the greatest amount of gas expansion, but we are limited as to the rate of this expansion; that is, we must not let it develop in the bore a pressure greater than fifteen tons in the gun-chamber or upon the interior walls of the piece. This is tantamount to saying that to produce maximum velocity we require the evolution, at a suitable limited rate of expansion, of the greatest possible volume of gas, the expansion of the gas constituting under these conditions the propelling impulse.

It may be stated here that we possess, *within limits*, the power of controlling the rate of combustion of colloid powders by varying certain conditions relating to combustion, the principal of which are (1) the size of the grains of which the charge is composed, (2) the volume of the powder-chamber, (3) the length of the bore of the gun, (4) the weight of the projectile. Granting, then, that we possess within limits the capability of controlling the rate of evolution of the powder-gases, we are led to the following conclusion: that the best smokeless powder is that stable colloid which, for a given weight of its substance, evolves in the bore of the gun at the most suitable rate of evolution and expansion, the greatest volume of gas, the said evolution being accompanied with the development of the least heat.

We are led by this deduction to regard the action of the powder from a new standpoint. Besides considering what a powder is composed of, we must now consider what gases it is converted into upon decomposition, and what volumes of these gases it generates. Most important of all, it leads us to conduct experiments for the purpose of ascertaining what colloid will, for a given weight of its substance, liberate the greatest volume of gases.

Here was one starting point for a series of experimental researches culminating in the discovery of an efficient smokeless powder. Another line of experimental approaches to the same end connected the efforts to toughen the substance of colloid films containing sufficient oxygen to effect their own complete combustion, with a view to the attainment of increased regularity in developed pressures; a third related to the determination of the causes of certain ballistic phenomena hitherto unexplained, e g., that acetone colloids developed, in some cases, greatly improved ballistic qualities, after the lapses of periods of from six to twelve months from time of manufacture. These several lines of experimental investigation proved in the end to converge towards the attainment of a common result—the development of a special form of nitro-colloid that possessed the toughness and therefore the regularity of burning of celluloid, and that contained enough oxygen to convert its substance, upon ignition, into wholly gaseous products—which the celluloid did not—and that liberated not only the greatest volume of powder-gases at the most suitable rate, but the greatest volume of gases that can be evolved by any colloid at any rate of combustion, whether these colloids contained or did not contain nitro-glycerin, metallic nitrates or other substances.

The questions now present themselves: in what ways do we possess the control of kind and amount of gases evolved upon the combustion of nitro-cellulose and of its colloids, how does the constitution of these gases vary; what are they?

It has been already stated that the exact chemical formulæ for cellulose and its nitro-derivatives have not yet been written. That for cellulose may be approximately expressed as $C_{6n}H_{10n}O_{5n}$, where n is an undetermined or indeterminate numerical quantity. When cellulose is steeped in nitric acid or in a mixture of nitric and sulphuric acids, it is converted into the substance the composition of which may be expressed as as $C_{6n}H_{10n-an}O_{5n}(NO_2)_{an}$. These two expressions, $C_{6n}H_{10n}O_{5n}$ and $C_{6n}H_{10n-an}O_{5n}(NO_2)_{an}$, may be considered in comparison with one another. But contain the same quantity of carbon; the quanti-

ties present of the other elements are changed by
nitration; *an* atoms of hydrogen are displaced by
an equivalents of a combination of nitrogen and
oxygen (NO_2). This additional oxygen from the
NO_2 acts to supply the energy that converts the
cellulose into an explosive, and enters into its substance in combination with a certain quantity of nitrogen. Why it carries the nitrogen with it we do not
know, but it is a chemical fact that it does so—the
fact upon which the designation of the new explosives as nitro-derivatives or nitro-explosives is
based.

Upon the ignition of the nitro-cellulose or its
colloid the nitrogen is set free; the hydrogen combines with its equivalent of oxygen and appears in
the air as steam; the remaining oxygen unites with
the carbon to form gaseous oxides of carbon. If
there be not enough oxygen to consume all the carbon into gas, part of the latter is deposited as soot;
this result was obtained in the attempt to employ
celluloid as gunpowder. If there is enough oxygen
to consume all the carbon into gases, we have, as
products of combustion, a mixture of the gaseous
oxides of carbon, of which there are two, CO_2 and
CO.

The property possessed by carbon of combining
at high temperatures with intense energy with
oxygen, to form gaseous oxides, is the fact upon
which the practical development of explosives depends; there are many explosives that contain neither

carbon nor oxygen, but with these we have as yet no practical relations in ordnance matters.

It has been stated already that the attempt to obtain what is called complete combustion for nitro-cellulose colloids by incorporating oxidizing agents into them had misled investigators, who confounded the attainment of complete combustion with the development of maximum velocity at lowest pressure. " Complete combustion " means the conversion of all the carbon into the higher oxide of carbon—carbonic acid, CO_2—a dense gas about 1.9 times as heavy as the air, the formation of which is accompanied with the development of a high degree of heat. The complete combustion of carbon into carbonic acid gas with the corresponding evolution of a great amount of heat is the characteristic of the combustion of nitro-glycerin. The lower oxide of carbon, CO, is a gas much less dense than carbonic acid, possessing a density of about 1.4 times that of air. Suppose that we have a given weight of a compound of carbon and oxygen, with the elements taken in such proportions as to produce, on ignition, complete combustion into carbonic acid gas, CO_2, with the accompanying evolution of a large amount of heat; let us also suppose that we have an equal weight of compound of the same elements in such proportions as to develop, on ignition, the lower oxide of carbon, carbonic oxide, CO; then, the latter compound, developing the lower oxide, would liberate a volume of gas nearly $1.9/1.4 = 1.36$ times greater than the former. The greater heat produced by the forma-

tion of the carbonic acid gas would cause the volume
of that gas evolved to be the more expanded, but,
at the same time, and this is a fact of crucial importance in the present work, the greater heat would
cause the gas to be generated at *a more rapid rate*,
in fact, at an extremely rapid rate; and what we require is a low, regular rate of gas evolution to prevent our exceeding at any time the set limit of permissible bore-pressure.

In our effort to generate from colloid nitro-cellulose the greatest volume of gas at the most gradual
rate of expansion, we must seek, then, (1) to avoid
the formation of CO_2 when CO may be formed in
lieu thereof; (2) to avoid the formation of free carbon; and (3) to generate the maximum volume of the
lower carbon oxide. If we give due consideration
to the amounts of water and of nitrogen formed
simultaneously with the oxides of carbon, we shall
find that the form of nitro-cellulose developing the
greatest volume of gas at the most suitable rate, corresponds to the formula $C_{30}H_{38}(NO_2)_{12}O_{25}$, which
breaks up on decomposition into $30\,CO + 19$
$H_2O + 12\,N$.

This material is a new type of nitro-cellulose,* developed by experiment to meet ballistic require-

---

* This special form of nitro-cellulose, which corresponds to a
content of nitrogen of 12.44 per cent, and which was first developed in Russia by the eminent chemist, Professor D. Mendeléef,
has been independently developed at the Torpedo Station,
through the study of effects of variation of times of immersion,
temperatures of nitration and of washing, and strength of acids
employed in the nitration of cellulose.

ments, which contains just enough oxygen to convert its substance into a gaseous body. Its formation from cellulose depends upon strengths of nitric and sulphuric acid, temperatures of reaction and time of immersion of the cellulose in the acids from which the material is prepared. With ether-alcohol it forms a colloid that possesses, on the one hand, the toughness, and therefore the capability of development of regular pressures, of celluloid; and on the other the capability of consuming into wholly gaseous products that characterizes the gun-cotton acetone colloid; while as a powder it develops, with present types of guns, excellent values of V/P of about 2400/16. Briefly, it may be described as a celluloid containing enough oxygen to convert its substance (when it is consumed out of contact with the atmosphere) wholly into gaseous products.

It was stated in a preceding paragraph that the ballistic effect produced by a progressive explosive depended directly upon the volume of gas it evolved upon combustion, but was not directly dependent upon the attainment of complete combustion. Assuming total conversion from solids into gases, and non-liability to detonation, pyrocellulose was shown to be the form of nitro-cellulose best adapted for conversion into smokeless powder. As this material contains only enough oxygen to convert its carbon into carbonic oxide, CO—less than gun-cotton, which converts its carbon partly into carbonic acid gas, CO_2, and partly into carbonic oxide, CO—the attainment of maximum efficiency from nitro-cellulose was thus shown to be accomplished through a reduction from a maximum to a mean in the quantity of oxygen capable of being incorporated into nitro-cellulose.

On the other hand, it was stated that the incorporation of certain quantities of oxygen-carriers (nitro-substitution compounds other than nitro-celluloses, such as nitro-glycerin and nitrates of metallic bases) into colloid nitro-cellulose, led to the attainment of an increase in initial velocity of projectile for a given developed bore-pressure. As nitro-glycerin furnishes a surplus of free oxygen to aid in completing the combustion of the gases from the nitro-cellulose, while the nitrates surrender oxygen on application of heat, it would appear in this case that the attainment of a more complete combustion led to improvement in ballistic effect.

We are thus brought face to face with a seeming contradiction—how, on the one hand, we must remove oxygen; how, on the other, we must add oxygen to a progressive explosive, in order to obtain maximum ballistic effect therefrom. In order to reconcile these apparently contradictory statements we must consider the manner of decomposition of the explosive in both cases.

One chief characteristic of pyrocellulose is its homogeneity. It represents no mixture of explosives and combustibles, such as are presented by other forms of powders, and it is converted directly by combustion into a set of gaseous decomposition products that may not be varied in amount and kind. Under these conditions the ballistic effect of the expanding gases from pyrocellulose may be referred to quantity of charge, area of ignition-surface, weight of projectile, calibre of gun, and volume of powder-chamber. Other conditions affecting developed pressure and velocity are bore-friction and resistance of the projectile to rotation through inertia.

The gun may be regarded as a gas-engine in which the walls of the chamber and bore form the cylinder; the projectile, the piston. The expanding powder-gases perform work by imparting velocity to the projectile, the inertia of which they overcome just as gas by its expansion in the cylinder overcomes the inertia of the piston and the parts linked thereto. In the engine the gas is admitted alternately, first at one end of the cylinder and then at the other; in the gun it is admitted in rear of the projectile but once, so that the gun is an engine of a single stroke. In the engine the steam is admitted into the cylinder through a valve, and, after the lapse of a period of time less than that required for a full stroke, admission is cut off and work for the rest of the stroke is performed expansively; in the gun the charge of powder constitutes both the gas itself and the valve that admits the gas—for each grain of powder may be considered as a notch of opening of a valve; the more grains there are the greater the ignition surface, the greater the rate of emission of gas, or the greater the number of notches the valve is open.

The action of nitro-cellulose powder-gases in imparting motion to the projectile is that of the gas in

the engine cylinder The decomposition products
are evolved at a high pressure, and act to propel the
projectile, just as the gas or vapor drives the piston
in an engine. Thus far the two cases are in parallel;
they differ in that the space occupied by the gas in
the gun is constantly increasing, both through the
effect of the motion of the projectile along the bore
and from the increase of chamber space due to the
melting away of the powder charge, while space in
the engine cylinder is increased through the motion
of the piston and through connection with the valve
before cut-off. As shown in Table I, the ballistic
value of gun-cotton colloided in acetone (for a given
gun) was$\dfrac{2100}{15-19}$; that of colloided soluble nitro-cellulose, containing not enough oxygen to convert its
carbon wholly into carbonic oxide, CO, was $\dfrac{2100}{16}$.
Under similar conditions of firing, pyrocellulose developed a value of $V/P = \dfrac{2400}{16}$. It may be urged
that the ballistic superiority of the latter colloid as
compared with that of the two former is not wholly
attributable to character and volume of evolved gases,
as the acetone colloid is brittle, and that prepared
from soluble nitro-cellulose is somewhat brittle, and
deficient in oxygen, while pyrocelluloid is of a tough,
leathery consistency, capable of withstanding high
pressures without premature disintegration. Nevertheless, as these colloids prove inferior to the pyro-
colloids for lower pressures of about 10 tons per

square inch, at which the effects of brittleness are not perceptible, and for which they all afford pressures regularly proportional to develop velocities, it remains that magnitude of volume of evolved gases is a factor of prime importance in the attainment of ballistic efficiency.

COMPOSITE POWDERS

The results of incorporating an oxidizing agent or oxygen-carrier into colloids merit special study. Suppose that a given nitro-cellulose be colloided and formed into strips of a number of definite thicknesses. If these strips be collected separately and dried, we may prepare from them series of rounds, each series composed of different weights of strips of some one thickness. If the length and breadth of the strips be great in relation to their thickness, we need consider only the latter element of dimension in relation to their mode of combustion.*

---

* We have (Glennon, Interior Ballistics, chap. VI, pp. 59, 60)

$$\phi(\gamma) = \alpha\gamma(1 - \lambda\gamma + \mu\gamma^2 \ldots),$$

where γ is the fractional part of the least dimension of the grain burned up to any moment, $\phi(\gamma)$ the fractional part of the whole grain burned up to the same moment; and α, γ, and μ, constants depending upon the form of the grain.

If the grain be a rectangular parallelopiped with a square base, and the altitude as the least dimension, we have

$$\alpha = 1 + 2x, \qquad \lambda = \frac{2x + x^2}{1 + 2x}, \qquad \mu = \frac{x^2}{1 + 2x},$$

where x is the ratio of the altitude to the side of the base."

Applying the above to the present case we find that if the alti-

Upon firing series of rounds of the several powders from a given gun we obtain the following results as to their manner of explosive action:

1.—Strips of over a certain mean thickness will be only partly consumed in the bore; the unconsumed remnants will be projected burning from the gun, to be quenched in the cool outer air, where they fall unconsumed to the ground and may be picked up at various distances from the piece in front of the muzzle, possessing the original form (in reduced dimensions) of the grains of which the charge was originally composed. Such powders develop low bore pressures and afford low muzzle velocities. In point of work performed they are equivalent to smaller charges of quicker powders. It may be remarked that no work is done in raising the temperature of the unconsumed portions of the grains, for if the temperature of the latter be raised but a few degrees, the ignition point of the explosive is reached and its substance would wholly disappear.

2.—Strips of under a certain mean thickness are totally consumed in the gun. They develop high pressures for low velocities. The thinner the strips the less the weight of charge required to develop the

---

tude be considerably diminished (x approaches zero) we have the case of the thin plate, and that the constants approach the values

$$\alpha = 1, \qquad \lambda = 0, \qquad \mu = 0,$$

or $\phi(\gamma) = \gamma$.

But γ depends alone on the thickness of the plate, therefore the speed of combustion of a plate is a linear function of its least dimension.

limiting permissible pressure, on account of the greater initial surface presented by the thinner strips, which occasions a high initial gas development.

3.—A certain mean thickness of strip will be found, for which, at a set limit of pressure, a minimum weight of powder will develop the greatest velocity that can be developed at that pressure. If strips of other thicknesses develop practically identical velocities and pressures for the same pressure limits, it will be by burning greater weights of powder. Such a powder may be designated a maximum powder, for the material from which it is prepared and for the gun from which it is fired.

Suppose, then, that colloided gun-cotton of nitration $N = 13.3$ develops in a given gun a maximum value $V/P = \dfrac{2100}{15}$, what will be the effect of incorporating into such powder a certain quantity of nitroglycerin, or of metallic nitrates such as barium and potassium nitrates? Assume that during the process of colloiding the requisite quantity of nitrates be uniformly incorporated throughout the substance of the pasty mass, which is subsequently formed into strips, as before. For this material we shall find that the maximum powder develops a value of $V/P = \dfrac{2400}{15}$, as against $\dfrac{2100}{15}$ for the pure colloid, a gain in velocity of 300 ft. sec. for a given pressure; in energy, $\left(\dfrac{mv^2}{2g}\right)$, of about 30 per cent.

If, in lieu of nitrates, we incorporate nitro-glycerin into the colloid, we will obtain a pasty mass that can be worked conveniently into the form of rods or cords, whence the name " cordite," applied to one of its best known types. Cordite, as used in England, consists of

> Nitro-glycerin ....58 parts
> Gun-cotton ....37 parts
> Vaseline .... 5 parts

Such a powder, fired under the above conditions, develops a value of $V/P = \dfrac{2400}{15}$ approx.

There is one characteristic of powders, such as the K and the French BN, containing nitrates, to which attention is to be directed. The nitrates contained in these powders exist in them in a state of suspension; in an undissolved state. For the BN the microscope reveals minute crystalline particles uniformly disseminated throughout its mass; the barium nitrate employed in the K powder is insoluble in the colloiding agent, acetone, and is also insoluble in the colloid, in which it is held in a state of suspension and of uniform distribution. ·

In the case of the nitro-glycerin powders it is known that the nitro-cellulose is not in true solution in the nitro-glycerin. In this connection the following quotation from an authority upon nitro-glycerin powders, Mr. Hudson Maxim, may be cited:

" In the very early smokeless powders, especially those made of compounds of soluble pyroxylin (gun-cotton) and nitro-glycerin, it was supposed that the nitro-glycerin actually held and retained the pyroxylin in solution, but it has since been learned that the nitro-glycerin is held by smokeless powders, whether made from high- or from low-grade gun-cottons, in much the same manner as water is held by a sponge; in fact, the pyroxylin exists in smokeless powders in the shape of a very minute spongy substance, and the nitro-glycerin is held in a free state within the pores of this sponge."

"It is possible even with powders containing as little as 25 per cent. of nitro-glycerin, to squeeze out the nitro-glycerin in a pure state by subjecting a piece of this powder to great pressure between smooth steel plates."

The quantity of nitro-carrier (nitrate or nitro-substitution compound other than nitro-cellulose) considered necessary to the production of good ballistic results, as exemplified in certain known powders, may be tabulated as follows:

TABLE III

Variety of Powder	Nitro-carrier used	Per cent. of Nitro-carrier in Given Wt. of Powder
Cordite.	Nitro-glycerin	58
Maxim	Nitro-glycerin	10 to 25
BN	Barium- and Potassium nitrates	21 to 25
K	Barium nitrate	14.25

The composition and ballistic properties of the three classes of explosives—pure colloids, colloids containing metallic nitrates, and colloids containing nitro-glycerin—may be compared as follows:

TABLE IV

Pure Colloid	K	BN	Cordite
Gun-cot- ton, 85.00 Soluble ni- tro-cellu- lose, 10.00 Sod. carb, 1.00 Solvent, res- ins, etc., 4.00 ——— 100.00	Gun-cot- ton and soluble nitro-cel- } 84.25 lulose, balanced Barium nitrate, 14.25 Calc. carb., 1.50 ——— 100.00	Insol. nitro- cellulose, 38.67 Soluble nitro- cellulose, 33.23 Barium nitrate, 18.74 Potassium nitrate, 4.54 Calc. carb., 3.65 Volatile, 1.29 ——— 100.12	Nitro-gly- cerin, 58 Gun-cot- ton, 37 Vaseline, 5 ——— 100

TABLE V

Type	Pure Colloid	Metallic Nitrate	Metallic Nitrate	Nitro-glycerin
Manner of incorporation of oxygen-carrier		Solid undissolved particles, uniformly distributed throughout colloid matrix	Solid undissolved particles, uniformly distributed throughout colloid matrix	Undissolved particles held in suspension like water in sponge
$\dfrac{V}{P}$	$\dfrac{2100}{15\text{-}19}$	$\dfrac{2400}{15}$	$\dfrac{2400}{15}$	$\dfrac{2400}{15}$

Remembering what has been said in relation to the ballistic performance of the varieties of powders cited, we are led to the following conclusion:

That minute particles of an oxygen-carrier uniformly incorporated into a nitro-colloid and held in suspension in an undissolved state throughout the body of the latter, render more progressive the combustion of the nitro-colloid into which they are incorporated.

For convenience of reference I shall refer hereafter to the oxygen-carrier held in suspension in the colloid as the *accelerator*. Viewed in the light of the principle here enunciated, the several powders we have been considering are all similar variants of the pure colloid. The remark of the compounder, " that a little nitro-glycerin certainly does help the powder along," is now the more readily comprehensible.

The methods commonly employed for co-ordinating natural species may be applied, by way of illustration, to the classification of the various types of progressive explosives, to establish their relations to one another, and to indicate the lines along which advances have been effected.

We shall next consider how the accelerator acts to develop increased velocity without developing increased pressure.

1.—It has already been shown how it is possible with powders containing as little as 25 per cent. of nitro-glycerin to squeeze out the nitro-glycerin in a pure state by subjecting the powder to great pressure between smooth steel plates.

If it be possible to extract nitro-glycerin by application of pressure from powder in which it is incorporated, then there will be a tendency to flow in the direction of least pressure from the instant of ignition of a charge to that of its complete combustion. This would mean, first, flow from within outwards in the

TABLE VI

PROGRESSIVE EXPLOSIVES

Family										
Genus	Agglomerated Powders		Pure Colloids				Accelerated Colloids			
Species	Black gunpowder	Brown powder	Acetone colloids (experimental, for small arms)	Pyrocellulose. United States, Russia, France	Acetic ether colloid, Wetteren	Ether-alcohol, with or without insoluble nitrocelluloses incorporated	Acetone colloid; nitro-glycerin accelerator	Acetone colloid of blended nitro-celluloses; barium nitrate accelerator	Ether-alcohol colloid; barium nitrate and potassium nitrate accelerator	Gun-cotton colloided with nitro-benzols
							Cordite Ballistite, Maxim	K.	BN. France	MN. Rifleite
Sub-species	Various mixtures of charcoal, saltpetre, and sulphur	Various mixtures of charcoal (partly charred and containing oxygen), saltpetre, and sulphur	Colloids of insoluble and soluble nitro-celluloses	Poudre B: France *	Gun-cotton, with or without soluble nitro-cellulose	From nitro-cellulose / From nitro-hydro-celluloses	Various proportions of nitro-glycerin in nitro-celluloses	Various proportions of nitro-celluloses and nitrates	Various proportions of nitro-celluloses and nitrates	*Rifleite;* nitro-cellulose colloided in acetone with or without dinitro-benzol
										Gun-cotton colloided with mono-nitro-benzol
Classification letter	A	B	C	D	B	F	G	H	I	J

* The first rational smokeless powder; developed in France by the eminent savant M. Vieille.

gun-chamber, where a relatively large proportion of the nitro-glycerin would be consumed; second, flow in the direction of the windage, where the quantity of nitro-glycerin consumed would also be relatively great. Such action accounts for the rapid erosion of the surfaces of gun-chamber and rifled bore when powders containing nitro-glycerin are employed.

2.—The eminent Russian chemist, Professor D. Mendeléef, developer of smokeless powder in Russia, in a paper upon pyrocellulose powder, says:

"The chemical homogeneity of pyrocollodion plays an important part in its combustion, for there are many reasons for believing that upon the combustion of those physically but not chemically homogeneous materials, such as nitro-glycerin powder (ballistite, cordite, etc.), the nitro-glycerin is decomposed first, and the nitro-cellulose subsequently in a different layer of the powder. The experiments of Messrs. T. M. and P. M. Tcheltsov at the Scientific and Technical Laboratory show that for a given density of loading the composition of the gases evolved by nitro-glycerin powders varies according to the surface area of the grains (thickness of strip), a phenomenon not to be observed in the combustion of the pyrocellulose powders. There is only one explanation for this, viz., that the nitro-glycerin, which possesses the higher rate of combustion (Berthelot), is decomposed sooner than the nitro-cellulose dissolved in it. This is the reason why nitro-glycerin powders destroy the inner surfaces of gun-chambers with such rapidity."

We conclude from the above that the nitro-glycerin incorporated into a colloid burns more rapidly than the nitro-cellulose forming the colloid. More nitro-glycerin is consumed with one part of the charge than with another. During the first period the products of combustion evolved in chamber and bore are largely those of nitro-glycerin; during the second, those of nitro-cellulose.

Moreover, as both materials exist in an uncombined state, although in one of intimate admixture; as both decompose wholly into gases, while each contains sufficient energy to continue its own decomposition, once that decomposition is begun, there is no reason why the rates of the two decompositions should be equal; it would rather appear that each substance should decompose at the rate peculiar to itself, so far as it was able, under existing conditions of heat and pressure, to effect a separation of its substance from the mixed mass of the powder.

Conditions point, therefore, to there being two intervals in the decomposition of the charge, during one of which a maximum quantity of nitro-glycerin, and, during another, a maximum quantity of nitro-cellulose is burning.

In what follows it is not intended to attempt more than to indicate the mode of progressive combustion as implying the superimposition of maxima and minima of effort. This may be represented graphically in the present case as follows:

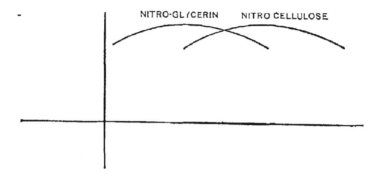

The result of the combination of the conditions here indicated would be the imparting of a double impulse to the projectiles due to the successive occurrence of two maxima of acceleration. Considered as to their limit of possible range, the successive impulses may occur incrementally, so that the accelerator may be expressed in the form

$$\phi\left(p'\right)\frac{d^2 p'}{dt^2} + \phi''\left(p''\right)\frac{d^2 p''}{dt^2},$$

where p' represents the pressure due at any instant to the combustion of the nitro-glycerin; p'', that due to the nitro-cellulose.

The projectile may be regarded as receiving a third impulse, resulting from the chemical combination of the gases evolved by the nitro-glycerin and the nitro-cellulose. According to the researches of Messrs. Macnab and Ristori (Proc. Royal Soc., vol. LVI, p. 8), the decomposition products of nitro-glycerin are

CO_2	CO	CH_4	O˙	H	N	H_2O.
57.6	—	—	2.7	—	18.8	20.7

And from the same source we obtain the decomposition products of nitro-cellulose (N $=$ 13.3) as

CO_2	CO	CA_4	O	H	N	H_2O
29.27	38.52	0.24	—	0.86	13.6	16.3

What may be called the third impulse would represent the combination at a high temperature of multiples of decomposition products developed in the ratios

$$A \begin{bmatrix} CO_2 & CO & CH_4 & O & H & N & H_2O \\ 57.6 & — & — & 2.7 & — & 18.8 & 20.8 \end{bmatrix}$$

$$B [29.27 \quad 38.52 \quad 0.24 \quad — \quad 0.86 \quad 13.6 \quad 16.3]$$

These phases may be indicated graphically as follows:

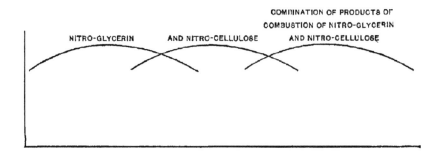

COMBINATION OF PRODUCTS OF
COMBUSTION OF NITRO-GLYCERIN
NITRO-GLYCERIN   AND NITRO-CELLULOSE   AND NITRO-CELLULOSE

Accelerated colloids of K and BN types containing metallic nitrates are next to be considered. We may assume that the nitro-colloid into which minute particles of a nitro-carrier of this type are cemented itself burns in approximation to the law of decomposition of the colloid. This state of affairs is similar to, though not identical with, the preceding; in the former, both nitro-glycerin and nitro-cellulose are able to effect their own decomposition, evolving gases that recombine; in the latter, the nitro-cellulose alone possesses this property, the metallic nitrates surrendering their oxygen through the effect of heat developed during decomposition of the colloid. The successive reactions may be represented as follows:

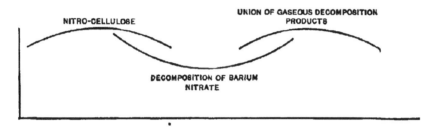

Instead of three maxima of effort there are two maxima and one minimum, the maxima representing the combustion of the nitro-cellulose and the subsequent combination of the gases therefrom with the oxygen of the barium nitrate; the minimum, the absorption of heat expended in decomposition of the barium nitrate.

A comparison of the diagrams shows that the processes of combustion in the case of colloids containing nitro-glycerin and of those containing metallic nitrates are similar. Both represent aggregates of work resulting from successions of independent decompositions. For such powders an element of time enters into our conception of chemical action; what the ultimate products of combustion are depends upon the order of occurrence of successive evolutions of various volumes of different gases at high temperatures.*

The base of the projectile is subjected to a series of impulses due to the development of successive waves of pressure, the result is an increased initial velocity for a given developed pressure, the acceleration being sustained throughout a comparatively longer period of time.

Those familiar with experimental development of ordnance during recent years remember a type of multi-charge gun the construction of which seemed based upon a favorable combination of correct principles, but which was rejected on trial, as its practical disadvantages were found to outweigh by far its advantages. I refer to the Lyman-Haskell multi-charge gun, a weapon supplied with a number of pockets distributed along the axis of the bore. In each pocket a charge of powder was placed; it was supposed that the projectile, by uncovering successive pockets in its flight, would cause their contents to ignite and thus furnish successive accelerating impulses to increase its velocity.

From what has been already said in relation to the principle of successive combustion, it will be seen that the employment of charges of accelerated powder, like those above described, in a gun of present-day type, represents the limiting extension of the multi-charge principle. In relation to their successive combustions, the nitro-glycerin and the nitro-

---

* See extracts from paper by Prof. Mendeléef, p. 33.

cellulose may be considered as sub-charges, contained in independent chambers or pockets, or distributed throughout a very large number of small pockets.

The principle already stated, as established by the study of the ballistic action of accelerated or composite powders, may be now amplified as follows:

Minute particles of an oxygen-carrier, uniformly incorporated into a nitro-colloid and held in suspension throughout the mass of the colloid in an undissolved state, act through their independent combustion in such a manner as to render more progressive the combustion of the colloid into which they are incorporated.